# EAT WHAT YOU WANT

## 125 RECIPES FOR REAL LIFE

Editor: Holly Dolce
Designer: Claudia Wu
Production Manager: Rebecca Westall

Library of Congress Control Number: 2019939747

ISBN: 978-1-4197-4286-6
eISBN: 978-1-68335-829-9

Copyright © 2020 Gaby Dalkin
Photography by Matt Armendariz

Cover © 2020 Abrams

Printed and bound in China
10 9 8 7 6 5 4 3 2 1

Abrams books are available at special discounts when purchased in quantity for premi-
ums and promotions as well as fundraising or educational use. Special editions can also
be created to specification. For details, contact specialsales@abramsbooks.com or the
address below.

Abrams® is a registered trademark of Harry N. Abrams, Inc.

**ABRAMS** The Art of Books
195 Broadway, New York, NY 10007
abramsbooks.com

What's Gaby Cooking

# EAT WHAT YOU WANT

## 125 RECIPES FOR REAL LIFE

Gaby Dalkin

PHOTOGRAPHY BY MATT ARMENDARIZ

ABRAMS, NEW YORK

# Contents

# Introduction

If you've been following along with me and my adventures, whether through my cookbooks, blog, social media, or all of the above, then you know that I'm all about food. I'm always thinking about what I'm going to eat. All. Day. Long. From waking up in the morning with a heaping slice of avo toast, to making a big bowl with all the toppings for lunch, to whipping up something simple and quick for dinner, and traveling all over the world looking for something new and delicious to eat. And why shouldn't I? It's something that brings me so much satisfaction and joy; it's something I get to share with my husband, Thomas, and all of our friends; and it's something that connects me with all of you. But lately I've been thinking about the questions that I've been getting more and more often from followers and friends alike: But what are you actually eating in real life? Or, But what are you eating when you want to feel great? Well, the answer to these questions is so important that it inspired me to write an entire book. Because the answer is simple: My food! My recipes! There is no alternate universe where I'm only drinking smoothies and eating skimpy salads (while I love a good smoothie and a salad, it's definitely not my style all the time). But let's get something straight, I'm also not eating the ENTIRE cheese board myself, and those desserts are typically being served up to a big crowd, including my friends and family. So bottom line, to everyone who has ever asked what I'm doing to look and feel good, I say this: It's all about balance, which means you can EAT WHAT YOU WANT.

That's why I wanted to devote this book to recipes that reflect how I eat in real life—no deprivation, no starvation, just my signature mash-up of bright flavors that are light and easy when you want it, and hearty and satisfying when you need it. And as always, simple enough to make during the week but special enough to serve up on the weekend. All of the dishes in this book will show you that you don't necessarily need to ditch the carbs/meat/dairy/sugar in order to feel awesome. How refreshing is that?!

I'm not a dietician, but I know a thing or two about the topic because . . . I eat for a living. Over the years, I've had a lot of time to think about what I'm choosing to put in my body

and how it makes me feel. What I've discovered is that I'm NOT a fan of diets (they never work for me!), and I think we will all drive ourselves crazy if we keep putting our favorite foods on the naughty list (who could actually live without bread or cheese?!). For me, balance really is everything. Sometimes we just need a little reset via lighter dishes filled with tons of fresh fruits and veggies like a Cauliflower Shawarma Bowl or lemony Tahini Broccolini. And then again, sometimes we just need a bowl full of Ham and Cheese Croissant Bread Pudding. And you know the recipes in this book are going to be solid, because if I'm going to invite a dish into my life, then it has to be the best of the best, epic of epic, ALL CAPS, everything. We're talking Bahn Mi Bowls that beat the best of takeout, and Sweet Potato–Black Bean Tacos that are so easy even Thomas could make them (a chapter in and of itself, because that guy is many things but a professional cook is not one of them—if he can do it, so can you!), and a Strawberry Crispy Cobbler that will make you weak in the knees. I'll also share some of my tried-and-true tricks of the trade for getting a delicious, filling, soul-nourishing meal on the table, like my favorite dishes for using up an over-ambitious farmers' market haul (since you know I can't control myself and always end up with more fruits and veggies than one human needs). And I've included an entire chapter of the best sauces and vinaigrettes for turning just about anything into a meal.

Plus, there's obviously going to be some menus to help you put together spreads for a crowd. When it comes to maintaining balance in my life, a crucial part of that is letting go and letting loose. I'm all about the Monday through Friday hustle, but when the weekend rolls around, I want to hit pause on the grind. Feeding my friends and family is one of my favorite things to do, especially because it means getting together, letting the week go, reconnecting, and recharging before we're back at it Monday morning. So what if that also includes a few bottles of rosé or a loaded-up cheese board? When you're giving yourself that kind of TLC—and rounding things out with dishes that feature lots of fresh seasonal produce—it does a body good. And because the weekend is also my favorite time to sneak in a hike, go for a bike ride, or get to my favorite workout class, I don't sweat it if my meals get a little indulgent. Whether you're planning a party or throwing together a pop-up feast, these menus are perfect for feeding a crowd and doing the weekend right. I designed them all so they can be tailored to your needs. So feel free to pick just a dish or two, or go all in and make the whole spread.

All told, *Eat What You Want* is an invitation/permission slip/pep rally for you to let go of all the noise around what you choose to eat. I say choose joy! Choose fun! Choose no apologies or excuses. But most of all, choose whatever makes you happy. I can't make that decision for you, but I can supply you with the recipes to make your journey that much more delicious. And I'll be here rooting you on—so go ahead and dig in!

# Chapter 1
# The Most Important Meal of the Day

Yes, yes, we all know that breakfast is the most important meal of the day. But before you roll your eyes and reach for that bar, think about how much better you feel when you have a full tank of (delicious) fuel before you dive into your jam-packed schedule. I know not every morning is going to be so leisurely and lovely, but that's why I've included lots of quick and easy recipes—sweet, savory, and everything in between—that you can make while half-asleep or even prep in advance. Then, when you have a little bit of time to stop and smell the pancakes, you can pick a recipe or two for a more laid-back brunch.

The recipes in this chapter also run the gamut from nourishing and fortifying to downright naughty. Because I think we can all agree that while most mornings a smoothie or loaded-up toast feels like the mature thing to do, sometimes self-care looks like a fresh batch of Ham and Cheese Croissant Bread Pudding. You know it's true!

# Blueberry Streusel Skillet
# Breakfast Cake

*Every once in a while something so simple and classic blows my mind with how impressive it can be. This super-moist, streusel-topped cake is just as perfect for a sophisticated brunch as it is made ahead and dished up for an on-the-go breakfast.*

---

### Ingredients

**For the streusel**

½ cup (110 g) packed brown sugar
¼ cup (30 g) all-purpose flour
Pinch of kosher salt
3 tablespoons unsalted butter, melted

**For the cake**

2 cups (250 g) all-purpose flour
1½ teaspoons baking powder
1 teaspoon kosher salt
½ cup (115 g/1 stick) unsalted butter, softened
1⅓ cups (265 g) sugar
2 large eggs plus 1 yolk
1 tablespoon vanilla extract
½ cup (120 ml) whole milk (or buttermilk if that's your jam!)
1 tablespoon fresh lemon juice
2 tablespoons lemon zest
2½ cups (365 g) fresh blueberries

**For the lemon icing**

1 cup (125 g) powdered sugar
2 tablespoons fresh lemon juice

Preheat the oven to 350°F (175°C). Spray a 9-inch (23 cm) cast-iron skillet with nonstick cooking spray.

To make the streusel: In a medium bowl, whisk together the brown sugar, flour, and salt. Add the melted butter and stir until a crumbly mixture forms with some large pieces still intact. Do not overmix.

To make the cake: In a small bowl, whisk together the flour, baking powder, and salt; set aside. In the bowl of an electric mixer, beat the butter until smooth, about 1 minute. Add the sugar and continue to beat, scraping down the sides of the bowl as needed, until the mixture is light and fluffy, about 2 minutes. Add the eggs and yolk and the vanilla and beat until combined. In two additions, add the milk and the flour mixture, alternating between the two. Beat until combined. Gently fold in the lemon juice, lemon zest, and blueberries. Transfer the batter to the prepared skillet and spread into an even layer. Sprinkle the top with the streusel. Bake on the center rack until a toothpick inserted into the center comes out clean and the topping is deep golden, about 50 minutes.

To make the icing: Meanwhile, in a small bowl, combine the powdered sugar with lemon juice and stir until smooth.

Transfer the skillet to a cooling rack and allow the cake to cool in the pan for about 15 minutes, then drizzle the top with the icing. Serve warm or at room temperature.

*Serves 8 to 10*

# *Ham & Cheese Croissant*
# Bread Pudding

*I mean . . . ham, cheese, croissants? Do I even need to explain? Probably not, but I'll just say that this is my take on the traditional ham-and-cheese-stuffed croissant, but all mussed up in a bread pudding—because who has time to be patisserie-perfect? It's a decadent morning treat, if I've ever seen one, and it's exactly what I reach for when I'm pulling out all the stops. It feeds a crowd, transports well, and the leftovers are next-level.*

---

### Ingredients

4 tablespoons (55 g) unsalted butter, plus more for greasing the pan

2 yellow onions, diced

2 tablespoons fresh thyme leaves, plus more for garnish

2 tablespoons Dijon mustard

Kosher salt and freshly cracked black pepper

8 large eggs

2 cups (480 ml) half-and-half

2 cups (220 g) grated Gruyère cheese

6 ounces (170 g) smoked ham, cut into 1-inch (2.5 cm) pieces

1 pound (455 g) croissants, ripped into 2-inch (5 cm) pieces (about 10 cups)

½ cup (50 g) grated Parmesan cheese

Flaky salt

Generously butter a 9 by 13-inch (23 by 33 cm) baking dish; set aside.

In a skillet over medium heat, melt the butter. Add the onions, reduce the heat to low, and cook until the onions are very soft and beginning to caramelize, about 10 minutes. Add the thyme, mustard, and salt and pepper and continue to cook, stirring occasionally, for 5 minutes more. Remove from the heat and let cool slightly.

In a large bowl, whisk the eggs and half-and-half until combined. Season with salt and pepper. Add the onion mixture, Gruyère, and ham, then add the croissant pieces and stir to coat them. Transfer the bread pudding mixture to the prepared dish, pressing it gently into the dish. Top with the Parmesan and cover with aluminum foil. Transfer to the refrigerator to chill for at least 1 hour or up to overnight.

When ready to prepare, preheat the oven to 350°F (175°C). Bake the covered bread pudding on the center oven rack for 30 minutes. Then uncover and continue to bake until the Parmesan has melted and turned golden, about 20 minutes longer. Allow to cool for 10 minutes, then serve warm with freshly cracked black pepper, flaky salt, and tons of fresh thyme.

*Serves 10*

# Soft Scrambled Eggs
## with Burrata on Toast

*Let's just all accept that I'm an elder millennial and breakfast toast is basically in my blood. If I'm not ordering avocado toast, then I'm going for this updated version with soft scrambled eggs spooned over a crusty slice of bread and topped with plenty of burrata cheese and herbs. It's as easy as it is delish.*

---

### Ingredients

4 large eggs

1 tablespoon unsalted butter

Kosher salt and freshly cracked black pepper

Snipped fresh chives

2 pieces crusty bread, toasted

1 ball burrata cheese

Fresh tarragon leaves

Flaky salt

In a medium bowl, crack the eggs and whisk them together. In a large nonstick skillet, melt the butter over medium-low heat. Once it is bubbling, carefully pour the eggs into the hot pan and season with salt and pepper. Slowly drag a spatula along the bottom of the pan allowing the eggs to cook slowly and evenly.

Once the eggs are cooked, season them with additional salt and pepper, depending on your preferences, and top with chives.

Divide the eggs between the 2 pieces of toasted bread. Add a spoonful of burrata on top of each one. Garnish with tarragon and finish with flaky salt and freshly cracked black pepper.

*Serves 2*

# Double Chocolate Chip
# Muffins

*I am not exaggerating when I tell you that growing up, I ate one enormous Costco double chocolate chip muffin. Every. Single. Morning. Okay, well technically I'd split one with my sister, but still. We'd microwave it just enough to get the chocolate chips nice and gooey (twenty seconds, to be exact), and then I'd try to steal the top of her half when she wasn't looking—because it's clearly the best part. After YEARS of experimenting, I finally nailed the re-creation of that muffin, which is basically cake in a muffin tin. But who cares? It's my childhood in edible form, and it's the best for breakfast.*

---

### Ingredients

1⅔ cups (205 g) all-purpose flour

¾ cup (75 g) unsweetened cocoa powder

2 teaspoons baking powder

½ teaspoon baking soda

1 teaspoon kosher salt

½ cup (120 ml) hot water

1 cup (200 g) sugar

⅓ cup (75 ml) vegetable oil

2 large eggs plus 1 yolk

2 teaspoons vanilla extract

¾ cup (180 ml) sour cream

2½ cups (435 g) semisweet chocolate chips

Preheat the oven to 375°F (190°C). Line a standard 12-cup muffin tin or a jumbo 6-cup muffin tin with paper liners.

In a bowl, whisk together the flour, ¼ cup (25 g) of the cocoa powder, the baking powder, baking soda, and salt; set aside. In a separate bowl, whisk together the remaining ½ cup (50 g) cocoa powder and the hot water until smooth.

In the bowl of a stand mixer fitted with a paddle attachment, beat the sugar, vegetable oil, eggs and yolk, and the vanilla on medium speed until combined, about 30 seconds. Add the cocoa powder mixture and beat until smooth. In three additions, add the flour mixture alternating with the sour cream until combined. Scrape down the sides of the bowl and add 2 cups (350 g) chocolate chips. Beat until just incorporated. Divide the batter evenly among the prepared muffin tin cups, filling the paper liners all the way up. Sprinkle with the remaining ½ cup (85 g) chocolate chips.

Bake in the center of the oven until the muffins have risen above the pan and a toothpick inserted into the center comes out clean, about 30 minutes for standard muffins, and 40 for jumbo.

Transfer to a wire rack to cool slightly before removing the muffins from the pan. Enjoy warm or at room temperature. Muffins can be stored in an airtight container at room temperature for 3 days.

*Makes 12 standard muffins or 6 jumbo*

# Banana Bread Pancakes

*Banana bread is one of my favorite sweet treats for breakfast. Thomas, on the other hand, always wants pancakes. So what's a girl to do? Come up with the ultimate mash-up! With this recipe, everybody wins. Note: The reason why I have you burying the chocolate chips is so that they don't get burnt and bitter. Plus, when you cut into the pancakes, there's a pocket of molten chocolate and banana—you're welcome!*

## Ingredients

1¾ cups (420 ml) buttermilk

¼ cup (60 ml) crème fraîche, stirred to loosen (or substitute Greek yogurt)

2 teaspoons vanilla extract

3 large eggs

¼ cup (55 g) unsalted butter, melted and cooled slightly, plus more for the pan

2½ cups (315 g) all-purpose flour

2 tablespoons sugar

1 teaspoon baking powder

½ teaspoon baking soda

½ teaspoon kosher salt

¼ teaspoon freshly grated nutmeg

4 bananas, peeled and roughly chopped

¾ cup (130 g) semisweet chocolate chunks

Maple syrup

In a small bowl, combine the buttermilk, crème fraîche, vanilla, eggs, and melted butter and stir until blended.

In a large bowl, whisk together the flour, sugar, baking powder, baking soda, salt, and nutmeg.

Pour the wet ingredients into the dry ingredients and whisk until a semi-lumpy batter forms; don't overwhisk. Let the batter rest for 10 to 15 minutes

Heat a nonstick skillet over medium heat, add 1 to 2 teaspoons of butter, then quickly wipe out the melted butter with a paper towel. Use a ¼-cup (60 ml) measure to scoop and pour the batter into the lightly greased pan, then sprinkle the pancake with a few slices of banana and chocolate chunks. With a small spoon cover the chocolate chunks with a little extra batter (this prevents the chocolate from burning when you flip the pancake). Cook for 2 to 3 minutes, until the edges start to bubble. Flip the pancake and continue to cook for another 1 to 2 minutes, until golden brown. Remove from the skillet. Pancakes can be kept warm in a low (225°F/110°C) oven, on a baking sheet fitted with a wire rack, until ready to serve. Repeat the process with the remaining batter.

Serve with warm maple syrup!

*Serves 8*

# Adam's Green Chile
# Cheddar Biscuits

*These buttermilk biscuits alone are worth making any time you have the chance, but adding some scrambled eggs and smoky chipotle gravy pretty much wins breakfast.*

---

## Ingredients

### For the buttermilk biscuits

2 cups (250 g) all-purpose flour, plus more for kneading

½ teaspoon kosher salt

4 teaspoons baking powder

¼ teaspoon baking soda

½ teaspoon freshly cracked black pepper

¼ cup (55 g) cold unsalted butter, cut into small pieces, plus 2 tablespoons melted butter

1 (4-ounce/115 g) can diced green chile peppers, drained

⅓ cup (45 g) small-dice Cheddar cheese

1 cup (240 ml) cold buttermilk

Flaky salt and freshly cracked black pepper

### For the chipotle gravy

6 ounces (170 g) pork or soy chorizo, removed from casing

2 chipotles in adobo, minced

2 tablespoons unsalted butter

2 tablespoons all-purpose flour

2 cups (480 ml) milk, warmed

2 tablespoons chopped fresh cilantro, plus more for garnish

9 large eggs

2 tablespoons olive oil

Kosher salt and freshly cracked black pepper

To make the buttermilk biscuits: Preheat the oven to 450°F (230°C).

In a large bowl, combine the flour, salt, baking powder, baking soda, and black pepper and gently whisk. Using a fork or a pastry cutter, cut the cold butter into the flour mixture until crumbly. Make a well in the center, place the green chiles and cheese in the well, and pour the buttermilk over the top. Carefully and slowly stir until the ingredients start to come together.

Turn the dough out onto a lightly floured surface and, with floured hands, give it a quick knead, 3 to 4 times, to bring it together. Pat the dough into an 8-inch (20 cm) square about 1 inch (2.5 cm) thick and cut into 9 square biscuits.

Place the biscuits on a baking sheet lined with parchment paper or a silicone mat, brush them with the melted butter, sprinkle with salt and pepper, and bake until the biscuits are puffed up and golden brown, 15 to 18 minutes. Transfer the biscuits to a wire rack to cool while you make the gravy and scrambled eggs.

To make the chipotle gravy: In a saucepan over medium-high heat, cook the chorizo and chipotles together for 5 to 7 minutes. Add the butter and stir until melted. Add the flour and cook for 1 to 2 minutes. Whisk in the milk and continue to stir. Bring to a boil so that the gravy will thicken, stir in the cilantro, and serve over biscuits.

Scramble the eggs. Cut the biscuits into halves, so you can sandwich equal amounts of the scrambled eggs between them. Drizzle with the gravy and garnish with cilantro.

*Serves 9*

# Avocado Migas

*I can't remember the first time I had migas, but it's safe to say that my life has never been the same. My guess is that it was on one of my road trips through the Southwest because that's usually where you can find this on the menu. It's traditionally scrambled eggs flavored up with veggies and cheese then finished off by tossing fried tortillas into the mix. Then I add tons of toppings like cotija cheese, refried beans, and avocado because there's nothing like a little breakfast fiesta.*

## Ingredients

2 tablespoons olive oil

6 small (6-inch/15 cm) corn tortillas, cut or torn into 1-inch (2.5 cm) pieces

1 small tomato, diced (roughly 1 cup/180 g)

½ yellow onion, diced (roughly 1 cup/110 g)

½ jalapeño chile, seeded and finely diced

4 large eggs

2 tablespoons milk

¼ teaspoon ground coriander

⅛ teaspoon ground cumin

Kosher salt and freshly cracked black pepper

1 cup (115 g) shredded Monterey or pepper Jack cheese

Refried beans and toast

### For the toppings

Sliced scallions

Chopped fresh cilantro

Diced avocado

Crumbled cotija cheese

Hot sauce

Heat 1 tablespoon of the olive oil in a large nonstick skillet over medium-high heat and fry the tortillas until crisp and lightly browned, about 5 minutes total, flipping the pieces halfway through. Remove the tortillas from the pan and set aside.

In the same skillet add the remaining 1 tablespoon of olive oil along with the tomatoes, onion, and jalapeño. Cook the vegetables until they are soft and excess moisture is cooked off, about 5 minutes.

While the tomato mixture cooks, whisk together the eggs, milk, coriander, and cumin in a bowl. Season with salt and pepper. Stir in half of the cheese.

When the tomato mixture is soft, return the fried tortillas to the pan and stir to combine. Reduce the heat to medium, pour the egg mixture into the pan, and stir with a spatula, slowly folding and moving the eggs around. Cook until the eggs are almost dry and fold in the remaining cheese. Remove from the heat. Serve with all the toppings and refried beans and toast on the side!

*Serves 2 to 4*

# Omelette Soufflé
## with Fontina & Herbs

*When I was growing up in Tucson, we'd sometimes go to our country club for break-fast where I would always hit up the build-your-own omelet station. I may have taken things a little too far with the fillings—we're talking piles of cheese and veggies—but hey, fair game! These days I'm stepping it up a notch with this omelet soufflé. It takes a little bit more effort to make than a traditional omelet, but I promise that all that fluffy, creamy, cheesy goodness is worth a little extra whisking.*

---

### Ingredients

3 large eggs, separated
1 tablespoon chopped fresh chives, plus more for garnish
1 tablespoon grated Parmesan cheese
Kosher salt and freshly cracked black pepper
2 tablespoons unsalted butter
3 tablespoons shredded Fontina cheese

In a medium bowl, beat the egg yolks, chives, and Parmesan and season with a pinch of salt and some pepper.

In a larger bowl, with a handheld mixer, beat the egg whites until they form stiff peaks.

Carefully fold half of the egg whites into the yolk mixture. Once combined, fold in the remaining egg whites and carefully mix until no streaks of egg whites remain.

Heat an 8-inch (20 cm) nonstick skillet with a fitted lid over medium-high heat. Melt 1 tablespoon of the butter in the pan and swirl to coat the bottom and sides. Pour the egg mixture into the pan and smooth the top with a spatula. Sprinkle the top with the Fontina.

Cover the pan with its lid and cook for 3 to 4 minutes; this will steam the top of the omelet and brown the bottom to a crispy golden brown.

After 3 to 4 minutes, remove the lid and use a rubber spatula to loosen the sides. Carefully fold the omelet in half and slide it onto a plate. Top with the remaining tablespoon of melted (on the stovetop or in the microwave) butter, extra chives, and more salt and pepper as needed. Serve immediately.

*Serves 1 or 2*

# Savory Dutch Baby

*As you can probably tell, I'm all about the savory breakfast. Give me eggs, bacon, and cheese and I'm a happy girl. That's why one of my favorite breakfast/brunch dishes is the Dutch baby, which is basically a giant popover that you can make extra savory with, you guessed it, eggs, bacon, and cheese, plus fresh herbs and pretty much any other topping your heart desires.*

---

Ingredients

For the Dutch baby

5 large eggs

1 cup (240 ml) milk

Pinch of sugar

9 tablespoons (125 g) unsalted butter, 5 tablespoons (70 g) melted and cooled

1 cup (125 g) all-purpose flour

½ teaspoon kosher salt

½ teaspoon freshly cracked black pepper

½ cup (50 g) finely grated Parmesan cheese

¼ cup (11 g) thinly sliced fresh chives

For the salad and fried eggs

1 tablespoon champagne vinegar

1 tablespoon fresh lemon juice

2 teaspoons whole-grain mustard

1 shallot, finely diced

3 tablespoons olive oil

Kosher salt and freshly cracked pepper

8 slices thick-cut bacon

5 ounces (140 g) market greens

4 eggs

To make the Dutch baby: Preheat the oven to 425°F (220°C). Once it comes to temperature, heat a 12-inch (30.5 cm) skillet in the oven for at least 20 minutes.

Meanwhile, combine the eggs, milk, sugar, melted butter, flour, salt, and pepper in a blender and blend till the batter is smooth with no lumps. Fold in the Parmesan and chives.

Once the pan is VERY hot, place the remaining 4 tablespoons (55 g) butter in the hot pan and leave the pan in the oven for about 3 minutes to lightly toast the butter. Using an oven mitt, grasp the skillet's handle and swirl the butter to make sure it evenly coats the pan. Quickly pour the batter into the hot pan and place it back in the oven. Bake the Dutch baby for 25 to 30 minutes, until it is puffed and very golden brown.

Meanwhile, prepare the salad and fried eggs: In a small mason jar, combine the vinegar, lemon juice, mustard, shallot, 2 tablespoons of the olive oil, salt, and pepper and shake to mix. Taste and adjust the seasoning.

Cook the bacon in a large nonstick skillet over medium-high heat until crispy and brown, then remove the bacon to a paper towel–lined plate. Once cool, crumble and set aside.

Just before serving, wipe out the skillet, add the remaining 1 tablespoon of olive oil, and fry the eggs until over easy. Remove them to a plate and season with salt and pepper. Toss the market greens in the vinaigrette, add the bacon, and toss again.

When the Dutch baby is done, either slide it out onto a serving platter or board, or serve it in the skillet. The popover will deflate as it cools. It can be served hot, warm, or room temperature. Top with the fried eggs and the salad.

*Serves 2 to 4*

# Smoothies
## for Every Mood

I couldn't promise you quick-and-easy breakfast options without including a few more smoothies to add into your rotation. These will hit the spot whether you're craving something rich and sweet, bright and fruity, energizing and green, or decadent and chocolatey.

1          2          3          4

# 1 Matcha Smoothie

### Ingredients

1 frozen banana, sliced (or use a fresh banana and add ⅓ cup/75 ml crushed ice)

¾ cup (480 ml) vanilla unsweetened almond milk

1 heaping teaspoon ceremonial grade matcha powder

1 to 2 Medjool dates (depending on your sweet preference), pitted

1 handful fresh spinach or kale leaves

2 teaspoons hemp seeds

Combine all the ingredients in a high-powered blender and blend for 1 to 2 minutes, until completely smooth and the hemp seeds are completely ground. Pour into a glass and drink up. *Serves 1*

# 2 South Beach Smoothie

### Ingredients

1 banana, sliced

1½ cups (360 ml) full-fat coconut milk

1 heaping teaspoon hemp hearts

1 heaping teaspoon chia seeds

1 teaspoon coconut butter

½ cup (85 g) frozen mango

½ cup (70 g) frozen raspberries

Combine all the ingredients in a high-powered blender and blend for 1 to 2 minutes, until completely smooth and the hemp hearts and chia seeds are completely ground. Pour into a glass and enjoy. *Serves 1*

# 3 Chocolate-Covered Strawberry Smoothie

### Ingredients

1 tablespoon cacao powder

1 tablespoon almond butter

¾ cup (180 ml) vanilla unsweetened almond milk

½ teaspoon chia seeds

½ teaspoon hemp hearts

1 cup (150 g) frozen strawberries

Combine all the ingredients in a high-powered blender and blend for 1 to 2 minutes, until completely smooth and the chia seeds and hemp hearts are completely ground. Pour into a glass and enjoy. *Serves 1*

# 4 Superfood Smoothie

### Ingredients

1 frozen banana, sliced

3 tablespoons almond butter

2 Medjool dates, pitted

1 tablespoon maca powder

2 tablespoons raw cacao nibs

1 teaspoon coconut butter

½ teaspoon bee pollen

1 cup (240 ml) vanilla unsweetened almond milk

Combine all the ingredients in a high-powered blender and blend for 1 to 2 minutes, until completely smooth and the cacao nibs are completely ground. Pour into a glass and enjoy. *Serves 1*

# *Austin-Style*
# Breakfast Tacos

*Every time we go to Austin, we head straight for breakfast tacos. It's a way of life there, and they've perfected the combination of doughy tortillas, fluffy eggs, cheese, and avocado. Lucky for you (and me), I've come up with a recipe that captures that same hand-held goodness—essential for when you need a hearty breakfast or you've had one too many margs the night before.*

---

## Ingredients

4 slices bacon

8 large eggs

2 tablespoons milk (or any unsweetened nut milk)

Kosher salt and freshly cracked black pepper

1 tablespoon unsalted butter

6 small flour tortillas

¾ cup (85 g) shredded Monterey Jack cheese

1 medium ripe avocado, pitted, peeled, and thinly sliced

Chipotle Salsa (page 252)

Fresh cilantro leaves

Finely chopped white onion

Lime wedges

Preheat the oven to 400°F (205°C). In a large nonstick skillet, cook the bacon over medium heat, flipping once, until crispy, about 5 minutes. Transfer to a paper towel–lined plate to drain, then break the slices in half.

In a medium bowl, beat the eggs with the milk and season with salt and pepper. Remove most of the bacon fat from the skillet and melt the butter in the remaining fat over medium heat. Add the eggs and cook, stirring frequently, until softly scrambled.

Turn on a gas burner to medium-high heat. Char each of the tortillas for 10 to 20 seconds per side, until just charred. Arrange the tortillas on a large baking sheet. Spoon equal amounts of the scrambled eggs onto each tortilla and sprinkle with the cheese. Bake for about 3 minutes, until the cheese is just melted. Top the eggs with the torn pieces of crispy bacon and the sliced avocado. Garnish with the salsa, cilantro, white onion, and lime wedges and serve immediately.

*Serves 2 to 3*

# Gaby's Bloody Mary

(or Maria)

*For those mornings when you need a little hair of the dog to get some pep back into your step.*

---

### Ingredients

6 ounces (180 ml) tomato juice

4 ounces (120 ml) vodka or tequila

10 shakes hot sauce

6 shakes Worcestershire sauce

1 ounce (30 ml) fresh lime juice

1 ounce (30 ml) fresh lemon juice

½ teaspoon freshly grated horseradish

¼ teaspoon smoked paprika

¼ teaspoon black pepper

2 tablespoons kosher salt

¼ teaspoon celery salt

### Assorted garnishes

Lime wedges

Lemon wedges

Celery stalks

Bacon

Mini gherkins

Pickled pearl onions

Cherry tomatoes

Castelvetrano olives

Cheddar cheese

Combine the tomato juice, vodka or tequila, hot sauce, Worcestershire, lime juice, lemon juice, horseradish, smoked paprika, and black pepper in a large shaker with ice and shake until well chilled.

Combine the kosher salt and celery salt; stir, then transfer to a small plate.

Run a lime or lemon wedge along the rim of 2 glasses, then dip the rim into the salt mixture to coat. Fill the glasses with ice and strain the Bloody Mary mixture into the glasses. Serve with desired garnishes.

*Serves 2*

# Chapter 2
# All About That Snack Life

What is life without snacks? With nothing to munch on throughout the day, things can get pretty grim between meals—and nobody wants that. That's why it felt like my responsibility to devote an entire chapter to them.
The recipes here will do the trick any time you need an appetizer, mini-meal, side, or an epic all-snack dinner (so pretty much any time). Combined with the recipes from my last book, I have you covered for any tasty bites and nibbles you could ever need.

# Chipotle Wings

*If it's game day, you can bet there's going to be a pile of wings coming out of my oven before all the guests arrive—especially these chipotle wings. Even if you don't consider yourself a traditional wing fan, these are the ultimate mind-changer. They're a little sweet, a little smoky, perfectly seasoned with a little zip from the lime, and endlessly snackable. Of course, if you want to partake, you'll have to join me in the kitchen, because there's no way I'm letting these saucy guys anywhere near my couch. Let's be honest, we all know the best part of game day is the food. Who needs a couch and TV?*

---

## Ingredients

2 pounds (910 g) chicken wings, trimmed into drums and winglets

Olive oil

Kosher salt and freshly cracked black pepper

1 tablespoon smoked paprika

3 cloves garlic

3 to 5 chipotle chiles in adobo plus about 4 tablespoons (60 ml) adobo sauce, depending on desired spiciness

2 tablespoons brown sugar

1 tablespoon Worcestershire sauce

2 tablespoons apple cider vinegar

6 tablespoons (85 g) unsalted butter

1 cup (240 ml) sour cream

Lime wedges

Fresh cilantro sprigs

Preheat the oven to 400°F (205°C). Line a rimmed baking sheet with aluminum foil and fit the pan with a baking rack.

In a large bowl, toss the wings with a generous drizzle of olive oil. Season with salt and the smoked paprika. Spread the wings on the rack on the baking sheet in an even layer. Bake on the top rack of the oven for 30 minutes. Turn the wings over and continue to cook for another 10 minutes.

Meanwhile, make the sauce. In the bowl of a food processor, combine the garlic cloves, chipotle peppers and adobo sauce, brown sugar, Worcestershire, and vinegar. Process until smooth. Season with salt and pepper. Transfer to a saucepan over low heat and add the butter. Cook until the butter is fully melted, whisking to combine. Toss the hot wings in the sauce and serve with the sour cream, lime wedges, and cilantro.

*Serves 2 to 4*

# Double Pea, Prosciutto &
# Burrata Platter

*When fresh peas hit the market, I'll put them on everything from pizza to pasta, bowls to salads, and I'll puree them into a pesto—anything to make the most of their all-too-short season. If I had to pick my favorite combination, though, it would be this super-simple DIY snack platter with prosciutto and burrata. Plus two kinds of peas, naturally. Serve with crostini, crackers, or just a spoon!*

---

### Ingredients

2 cloves garlic, finely chopped

⅓ cup (30 g) finely grated Pecorino Romano cheese, plus more for finishing

⅓ cup (75 ml) extra-virgin olive oil

Juice of 1 lemon

¼ teaspoon red pepper flakes

Kosher salt and freshly cracked black pepper

1 (10-ounce/280 g) package frozen peas, completely thawed

½ cup (135 g) thinly sliced sugar snap peas

4 ounces (115 g) thinly sliced prosciutto

6 ounces (170 g) burrata cheese

Fresh dill fronds

Toasted crostini or crackers

Put the garlic in a medium bowl and add the Pecorino, a few tablespoons of the olive oil, the lemon juice, red pepper flakes, salt, and plenty of black pepper and whisk to combine. Add half of the thawed peas and the sliced sugar snap peas. Taste and adjust the salt and pepper as needed.

Using the back of a fork, roughly mash the rest of the peas so they are a little more chunky and add them to the bowl, stirring to combine. Transfer the pea mixture to a serving platter. Scatter the sliced prosciutto on top and tear the burrata and scatter that on top as well. Garnish with fresh dill fronds and serve with crostini or crackers.

*Serves 4 to 6*

# Bacon
# French Onion Dip

*Who on earth is going to tell you to go buy almost three pounds worth of onions and shallots and turn them into a dip? That's right, it's me. Hey, you trusted me when I told you you needed to peel your chickpeas for the perfect hummus! So trust me again on this one . . . it's worth it. This is an elevated version of French onion dip, and I can promise that you'll never go back to making it any other way—or buying it from the store—ever again.*

---

### Ingredients

¼ cup (60 ml) olive oil

2 pounds (910 g) large yellow onions, thinly sliced

3 large shallots, thinly sliced

4 sprigs thyme

Kosher salt and freshly cracked black pepper

1 cup (240 ml) white wine

2 tablespoons champagne vinegar

2 cups (480 ml) sour cream

½ cup (30 g) chopped fresh chives, plus 2 tablespoons for garnish

4 strips cooked bacon, roughly chopped

¼ cup (60 ml) plain Greek yogurt

Juice of 1 lemon

Everything seasoning

Potato chips of your choice

In a large skillet, heat the olive oil over medium-high heat. Add the onions, shallots, and thyme sprigs and season with salt and pepper. Sauté for 10 to 15 minutes, until the vegetables start to caramelize. Reduce the heat to medium and continue to caramelize for a total of 35 minutes, until the onions and shallots are deep golden brown and caramelized.

Discard the thyme sprigs. Pour the wine and vinegar into the skillet and stir to scrape up any browned bits from the bottom of the pan. Continue to cook, stirring occasionally, about 15 minutes longer, until the liquid has evaporated. Spread the onion mixture out on a rimmed baking sheet to cool.

Transfer the onion mixture to a medium bowl. Stir in the sour cream, chives, bacon, yogurt, and lemon juice. Season with salt and everything seasoning. Garnish with the remaining 2 tablespoons of chives and serve with your favorite potato chips.

*Serves 4 to 6*

# *Whipped Goat Cheese &*
# Crudités

*When the farmers' market season is in full swing and my fridge is bursting with gorgeous veggies, I'm always making this dip to pair with an easy app, or throwing in Hummus and Green Goddess Dip (both in my last cookbook) for a crowd pleasing crudité platter.*

---

### Ingredients

11 ounces (310 g) goat cheese

3 tablespoons whipped cream cheese

2 cloves garlic

½ teaspoon red pepper flakes

Zest of 1 lemon

1 teaspoon fresh thyme leaves

Kosher salt and freshly cracked black pepper

Crostini

### For the crudités

Persian cucumbers, quartered lengthwise

Snap peas

Endive, peeled into individual leaves

Baby bell peppers

Baby heirloom carrots

Breakfast radishes, whole

Watermelon radishes, sliced

In the bowl of a food processor, combine the goat cheese, cream cheese, garlic, red pepper flakes, lemon zest, and thyme leaves. Whip for 60 to 90 seconds, until smooth. Taste and season with salt and pepper as needed. Serve with the crostini and crudités.

*Serves 4 to 6*

# Baked Feta
## with Honey & Black Pepper

*Normally when I bake cheese, I go for a gooey, melty, pull-apart variety. But I was recently turned on to baked feta and have never looked back. It gets soft and creamy but still keeps all that salty brininess. Paired with black pepper and honey, it's a match made in appetizer heaven.*

---

### Ingredients

1 (8-ounce/225 g) slab Greek feta cheese, blotted dry

2 tablespoons olive oil

1 tablespoon honey

Freshly cracked black pepper

Fresh thyme leaves

Toasted crostini

Preheat the oven to 400°F (205°C).

Place the feta in a small baking dish and drizzle olive oil over the top. Bake until the cheese is soft and springy to the touch but not melted, about 8 minutes.

Remove the feta from the oven and preheat the broiler. Drizzle the honey over the top and sides of the feta, and then broil until the top of the cheese browns and just starts to bubble, 2 to 3 minutes.

Remove from the oven, season with plenty of freshly cracked black pepper, and garnish with thyme. Transfer the feta to a serving dish and serve immediately with crostini.

*Serves 2 to 4*

# *Parmesan Pizza* Popcorn

*I recently had my wisdom teeth pulled (no, I didn't get them out until I was in my thirties; yes, I'm a late bloomer), and even though I was dreading it, the surgery and recovery weren't as bad as I was expecting. That's mainly because I had a bit of a love affair with Pirate's Booty, that puffed cheesy snack that melts in your mouth and is perfect for eating when you can't really chew. It was a full-on obsession that reignited my love affair with popcorn, so I've been making my own jazzed-up versions ever since. Put out a bowl of this homemade air-popped popcorn with cheesy Italian-flavored seasoning, and you'll have the ultimate munchie for game day or movie night.*

---

## Ingredients

6 tablespoons (85 g) unsalted butter
1 teaspoon dried oregano
1 teaspoon garlic salt
1 teaspoon dried basil
1 teaspoon dried thyme
1 teaspoon dried parsley
½ teaspoon flaky sea salt
½ teaspoon dehydrated ground onion
½ teaspoon red pepper flakes
½ teaspoon dried rosemary
4 tablespoons (60 ml) olive oil
½ cup (225 g) popcorn kernels
¾ cup (70 g) grated Parmesan cheese

In a small saucepan, melt the butter over medium heat. Add the oregano, garlic salt, basil, thyme, parsley, sea salt, ground onion, red pepper flakes, and rosemary and stir to combine. Let the mixture simmer for 2 to 3 minutes to infuse the butter and then remove from the heat and set aside.

In a large saucepan, heat 2 tablespoons of the oil over medium-high heat. Add the popcorn kernels to the hot oil and cover the saucepan with a lid. Gently shake the saucepan by moving it back and forth over the heat source. Once the kernels start popping, continue to shake the pan until the popping stops. Remove the pot from the heat, pour the spiced butter mixture over the popped corn along with the grated Parmesan and the remaining olive oil, and toss to combine. Add more salt if needed and serve.

*Serves 6+*

# Hummus
## *with Spiced Cauliflower*

*I love a lamb / hummus combo, but I know it isn't everyone's cup of tea, so I took the warm and smoky flavors from the meat and slathered them over some cauliflower rice instead. The whole thing gets stuffed into or on top of a pita. So good. And don't shy away from the cinnamon in the topping—trust me, it works!*

---

### Ingredients

**For the cauliflower topping**

1½ tablespoons olive oil

1 yellow onion, thinly sliced into half-moons

Kosher salt

1 clove garlic, minced

1¼ pounds (570 g) cauliflower rice

Freshly cracked black pepper

1½ teaspoons ground cumin

¾ teaspoon ground cinnamon

1 teaspoon ground coriander

½ teaspoon ground cardamom

¼ teaspoon cayenne, plus more if you want it spicier

2 tablespoons tomato paste

1 tablespoon balsamic vinegar

**For the hummus**

1 (15-ounce/430 g) can chickpeas, drained and peeled

½ cup (120 ml) tahini

2 to 3 tablespoons fresh lemon juice, plus more as needed

2 to 3 small cloves garlic

¾ teaspoon kosher salt, or more to taste

**For serving**

Fresh parsley leaves, chopped

Olive oil

**To make the cauliflower topping:** In a large skillet, heat the olive oil over medium heat. Add the onions and stir to coat in the oil. Spread the onions evenly in the pan and sprinkle with a pinch of salt. Cook over medium heat, stirring occasionally, until the onions are golden brown and begin to caramelize, about 10 minutes. If they start cooking too quickly or seem dry, reduce the heat and add a splash of water. Add the garlic and cook until fragrant, about 1 minute.

Add the cauliflower rice and season with 1 teaspoon salt and some pepper and stir to combine. Add the spices, tomato paste, and balsamic vinegar, stir to combine, and scrape up any brown bits from the bottom of the pan. Cook for about 3 minutes, until the cauliflower is fully seasoned and starts to caramelize. Taste and adjust the seasoning. Remove the pan from the heat and cover to keep the cauliflower warm.

**To make the hummus:** In a food processor, blend the chickpeas by themselves for 1 minute, until powdery clumps form. Scrape down the sides and blend again until everything is the same consistency. Add the tahini, lemon juice, garlic, and salt and blend until smooth. With the machine running, drizzle in 1 tablespoon of water at a time (1 to 3 tablespoons is usually all you will need), until you get a very smooth, light and creamy mixture. Taste and adjust the seasonings, adding more salt, garlic, or lemon juice if needed.

To serve, scoop the hummus onto a platter. Sprinkle the hummus with the cauliflower topping and parsley. Drizzle with olive oil and serve with pita chips.

*Serves 4 to 6*

# Make a Mezze

Inspired by my trip to Morocco, this menu is your guide for putting together a traditional mezze spread, or a buffet with lots of little sides and salads that everyone can use to dip and schmear to their heart's content.

---

Chicken and Beef Kefta
Garlic Flatbread
Shirazi-Style Salad
Papa's Eggplant Dip
Spicy Feta Dip
Tahini Cauliflower
Muhammara
Zegroni

*Serves 6 to 8*

# Chicken & Beef Kefta

## Ingredients

2 medium zucchini

3 teaspoons kosher salt

⅔ cup (35 g) sliced scallions

⅔ cup (35 g) chopped fresh mint

6 tablespoons (15 g) chopped fresh cilantro

6 cloves garlic, finely chopped

2 teaspoons ground cumin

2 teaspoons ground coriander

¼ cup (60 ml) tahini

1 pound (455 g) ground chicken (white or dark meat)

1 pound (455 g) ground beef (85% lean)

24 small wooden skewers, soaked in water for 20 minutes

Grate the zucchini, combine it with 1 teaspoon of the salt, and let sit for 5 minutes. Squeeze out as much liquid as possible. In a large bowl, mix together the zucchini with the scallions, mint, cilantro, garlic, cumin, coriander, remaining 2 teaspoons salt, and the tahini. Divide the zucchini mixture into 2 bowls. Mix the chicken into one bowl until well combined and the beef into the other.

Divide the chicken mixture into 12 pieces, then with damp hands, shape each piece around a soaked skewer into a sausage-like shape—round and roughly 5 inches (12 cm) long. Repeat the same process for the beef skewers.

Heat a large flattop grill pan over medium-high heat. Working in batches, brush the kebabs with a bit of oil, then grill them for 8 to 10 minutes on each side, until cooked through. Serve immediately.

# Garlic Flatbread

**Ingredients**

2 teaspoons active dry yeast

2 teaspoons sugar

¾ cup (180 ml) warm water (about 100°F/38°C)

4 cups (500 g) all-purpose flour, plus more for dusting

1 tablespoon fine sea salt

¼ teaspoon baking powder

6 tablespoons (90 ml) plain Greek yogurt

¼ cup (60 ml) olive oil

½ cup (120 ml) melted butter mixed with 8 cloves minced garlic

Kosher salt

**For serving**

Assorted olives

Assorted pickled vegetables

Store-bought labneh or other thick Greek yogurt

Hummus (page 51)

Lemon Tahini Dressing (page 252)

In a large glass, dissolve the yeast and 1 teaspoon of the sugar with the warm water. Let it sit on your counter until the yeast is frothy, about 10 minutes.

Meanwhile, sift the flour, salt, remaining 1 teaspoon of sugar, and baking powder into a large, deep bowl.

Once the yeast is frothy, add the yogurt and olive oil to the glass and stir to combine. Pour the yogurt mixture into the dry ingredients and gently mix together with a fork. When the dough is about to come together, use your hands to mix. As soon as it comes together, stop kneading; it should feel a bit sticky. Cover the dough with plastic wrap and let it sit in a warm, draft-free place for 3 hours.

After 3 hours, assemble two bowls, one with some extra flour and one with water. The dough will still be sticky. Separate the dough into six equal portions and lightly roll each one in the bowl of flour to keep them from sticking to each other. Using a rolling pin, roll each piece of dough into a circle about ¼ inch (6 mm) thick.

Warm a large cast-iron skillet over high heat until it's nearly smoking. Make sure you have a lid large enough to fit the skillet and place the bowl of melted garlic butter nearby.

Dampen your hands in the bowl of water and pick up one of your circles of dough, flip-flopping it from one hand to the other to lightly dampen it. Gently lay it in the skillet and set your timer for 1 minute. The dough should start to bubble. After about 1 minute, flip the flatbread; it should be blistered and somewhat blackened. Cover the skillet with the lid and cook for about 1 minute more.

Remove the flatbread from the skillet, brush with a bit of garlic butter, and sprinkle with a little kosher salt. Place the seasoned flatbread in a tea towel–lined dish. Repeat with the rest of the dough and serve warm with your choice of suggested accompaniments.

# Shirazi-Style Salad

### Ingredients
1 large yellow onion, thinly sliced

3 to 4 large heirloom tomatoes, sliced

1 pint (300 g) baby cherry tomatoes

4 Persian cucumbers, sliced in half lengthwise and then crosswise into ½-inch (12 mm) pieces

1 red bell pepper, seeded and cut into 1-inch (2.5 cm) pieces

3 tablespoons olive oil

1 tablespoon red wine vinegar

1 tablespoon fresh lemon juice

¼ cup (11 g) chopped fresh chives

¼ cup (13 g) chopped fresh dill

3 tablespoons chopped fresh parsley

3 tablespoons fresh mint leaves

2 tablespoons fresh tarragon leaves

Kosher salt and freshly cracked black pepper

Combine all the ingredients together in a bowl and toss to evenly mix. Keep in the fridge for up to 4 hours, until ready to serve.

# Papa's Eggplant Dip

### Ingredients
1½ pounds (680 g) eggplant

2 green bell peppers

3 tablespoons olive oil

2 firm-ripe Roma tomatoes, seeded and finely chopped

3 tablespoons chopped fresh parsley

2 cloves garlic

2 tablespoons red wine vinegar

¾ teaspoon kosher salt, plus more to taste

Freshly cracked black pepper

Broil the eggplant and bell peppers until blackened. Transfer to a heatproof bowl and cover with plastic wrap to steam for 10 minutes. When cool enough to handle, remove and discard the skins.

Transfer the eggplant and pepper flesh to a food processor or blender and blend until smooth. Slowly pour in the olive oil through the food chute and process until well incorporated.

Add the tomatoes, parsley, garlic, vinegar, and salt and pulse a few times. Season the dip to taste with more salt and some black pepper. Serve at room temperature.

# Spicy Feta Dip

**Ingredients**

1 (14-ounce/400 g) package feta cheese, packed in brine

¼ cup (60 ml) extra-virgin olive oil, plus more for drizzling

1 small pasilla chile, roughly chopped

1 serrano chile, roughly chopped

1 jalapeño chile, roughly chopped

Juice of half a lemon

¼ teaspoon dried oregano, plus fresh oregano for garnish (optional)

Freshly cracked black pepper

Remove the feta from the brine and pat it dry with paper towels. Crumble the feta into a medium bowl and set aside. Combine the olive oil, chile peppers, and lemon juice in a blender and blend until no more chunks remain. Taste and add more chile peppers if you want it spicier. Stir the chile pepper mixture into the crumbled feta and season with the dried oregano and black pepper to taste.

Cover and refrigerate overnight to allow the flavors to come together. When you are ready to serve, drizzle with more olive oil and garnish with fresh oregano if desired.

# Tahini Cauliflower

**Ingredients**

3 to 4 bunches cauliflower florets, broken into small pieces

3 tablespoons olive oil

Kosher salt and freshly cracked black pepper

1 teaspoon ground cumin

½ teaspoon red pepper flakes

½ cup (120 ml) Lemon Tahini Dressing (page 252), plus more as needed

Preheat the oven to 450°F (230°C). Line a baking sheet with parchment paper or aluminum foil. Spread out the cauliflower evenly on the baking sheet and drizzle with the olive oil.

Using tongs, gently toss the florets in the oil to coat and season with salt and pepper, the cumin, and red pepper flakes. Roast for 25 to 35 minutes until the cauliflower is just golden and slightly crispy. While the cauliflower is still hot, drizzle the lemon tahini dressing on top. Toss to combine and serve as needed.

# Muhammara

### Ingredients
1 cup (120 g) raw cashews
3 roasted red bell peppers
1 teaspoon red pepper flakes
1 teaspoon cayenne pepper
1 teaspoon ground cumin
1 shallot, roughly chopped
2 cloves garlic, minced
1 tablespoon pomegranate molasses
1 tablespoon fresh lemon juice
Kosher salt and freshly cracked black pepper
2 tablespoons olive oil

Combine all the ingredients in a food processor and blend until smooth. Adjust the seasoning if needed. Serve at room temperature.

# Zegroni

### Ingredients
5 ounces (150 ml) rye
5 ounces (150 ml) bourbon
10 ounces (300 ml) campari
10 ounces (300 ml) sweet vermouth
Orange peels

Pour the rye, bourbon, campari, and vermouth into a large pitcher and stir to combine. Chill until ready to serve. Serve over ice with an orange peel for garnish.

## Chapter 3
# Eat Your Greens

I live for salad—but not because it's "healthy" or "good."
I love it because it's the ultimate dish for mixing and match-
ing flavors, layering ingredients, and piling a whole bunch of
deliciousness in a bowl and digging in with reckless abandon.
The key to a great salad is fresh produce; plenty of add-ins;
and a bright, balanced dressing. The recipes in this chapter
will get you there! I also threw in a few soups, because they,
too, are an amazing and tasty way to get in lots of veggies
with delicious, layered flavors. And because more is more!

# Raw Corn, Zucchini &
# Snap Pea Salad

*It seems like every time I post a new recipe using raw corn, I get countless messages from people asking, "Are you sure you're supposed to use raw corn?!" So here's the answer once and for all: Yes! Raw corn is incredible; when it's in season, it has a deliciously sweet flavor and a crunchy texture. And it's what makes this light, bright summertime salad really shine.*

---

### Ingredients

3 ears corn

8 ounces (225 g) stringless snap peas

2 zucchini

2 watermelon radishes

¼ cup (13 g) chopped fresh mint

2 tablespoons chopped fresh chives

Sea salt and freshly cracked black pepper

Lemon Vinaigrette (page 255)

Cut the corn away from the cob and put the corn kernels in a large bowl.

Trim the ends off the snap peas and then separate lengthwise into halves. Add the sliced snap peas to the bowl of corn.

Slice the zucchini on a mandoline or run them through a spiralizer. Add to the bowl.

Thinly slice the radishes and add to the bowl. Add the fresh mint and chives and season with salt and pepper. Toss with the vinaigrette and transfer to a platter to serve.

*Serves 4 to 6*

# Stone Fruit Panzanella
## *with Burrata*

*It's almost embarrassing how much stone fruit I bring home from the farmers' market every week. Seriously, it's slightly beyond what a human should be able to consume. But when peaches, plums, and nectarines are as sweet and juicy as they are in the summer, I think it's my duty to eat as much of them as I possibly can. In order to do just that, I came up with this salad with two versions, both of which celebrate that special moment in time when summer produce is in peak season. All that natural perfection doesn't need much more than a light vinaigrette, some crunchy croutons, and creamy burrata.*

---

### Ingredients

2 nectarines, pitted and cut into wedges

2 plums, putted and cut into wedges

2 peaches, pitted and cut into wedges

1 cup (105 g) Rainier cherries or other sweet variety, pitted and halved

1 to 2 medium heirloom tomatoes, cut into wedges

½ cup (75 g) heirloom cherry tomatoes

Homemade Chunky Garlic Bread Crumbs (page 256)

8 to 12 ounces (225 to 340 g) burrata cheese, torn into bite-size pieces

Maldon sea salt and freshly cracked black pepper

Basil Vinaigrette (page 254)

Fresh basil leaves

In a large bowl, arrange the fruit, tomatoes, bread crumbs, and pieces of burrata cheese. Season with salt and pepper and drizzle with the basil vinaigrette. Top with basil leaves.

*Serves 4 to 6*

# *Heirloom Tomato & Steak*
# Caprese

*Whenever tomato season hits, it's my time to shine. I buy ALL the heirloom tomatoes, then once I get them home, I figure out different ways to use them. A simple caprese salad with mozzarella and basil is my usual choice, but Thomas doesn't consider that dinner. Add some steak though, and you've got yourself a meal. Steak caprese, all summer long.*

---

### Ingredients

¼ cup (60 ml) olive oil

¼ cup (60 ml) red wine vinegar

2 cloves garlic, chopped

1 teaspoon dried basil

1 teaspoon dried thyme

1 teaspoon dried dried oregano

1 pound (455 g) hanger or skirt steak

2 pounds (910 g) heirloom tomatoes, both regular and cherry, halved and quartered

¼ red onion, thinly sliced

6 ounces (170 g) fresh mozzarella, torn into bite-size pieces

Basil Vinaigrette (page 254)

Kosher salt and freshly cracked black pepper

In a large nonreactive bowl, combine the olive oil, vinegar, garlic, basil, thyme, and oregano and stir. Remove half of the marinade to another bowl. Add the steak to one bowl and marinate for at least 2 hours. Add the tomatoes and red onion to the other bowl and toss to combine. Set aside.

When you're ready to cook, heat a grill over medium-high heat. Shake excess marinade off the meat and generously season it with salt and pepper. Place the steak on the grill and cook until medium or medium rare, 4 to 6 minutes on each side, depending on your preference. Remove the meat to a cutting board and let rest for 10 minutes.

Transfer the tomatoes and red onion with all the marinade to a serving platter and nestle in the torn cheese. Slice the steak against the grain and nestle the slices into the tomato salad. Drizzle with the basil vinaigrette and season with salt and pepper as needed. Serve immediately.

*Serves 4 to 6*

# *Asian*
# Cucumber Salad

*If you've read my second cookbook,* What's Gaby Cooking, *then you're already aware that my mom makes the best cucumber salad on the planet. This recipe is my spin on that hard-to-top staple; I gave it an Asian twist that makes it perfect for adding to poke bowls, as a side salad for sushi, or just for serving up alongside some ribs.*

---

## Ingredients

1 pound (455 g) Persian cucumbers

Asian Vinaigrette (page 253)

1 ripe avocado, pitted, peeled, and sliced or diced

2 cups (60 g) loosely packed mâche lettuce

Gently smack the cucumbers with a rolling pin or the bottom of a heavy pot until they begin to break apart. Tear them into bite-size pieces.

In a medium bowl, whisk the ingredients for the dressing. Taste and adjust the salt as needed. To the same bowl, add the avocado, smashed cucumbers, and mâche and toss to combine. Serve immediately.

*Serves 4 to 6*

# The LA Chop

*If you've ever ordered a salad in Los Angeles, then chances are you've had "the chop." The restaurant Mozza made it famous, and now pretty much every restaurant in the city offers their spin. Once you try it, you'll know why—it's the perfect balance of flavors, the perfect combination of ingredients, and it has the perfect texture, thanks to everything being chopped up and tossed together. I had to come up with my own version out of necessity because I can never get enough of this salad, but now I can have it at home any time the craving strikes. And guess what? Mine goes heavy on the cheese.*

### Ingredients

Lemon Vinaigrette (page 255) with 2 tablespoons dried oregano mixed in

Kosher salt and freshly cracked black pepper

1 head iceberg lettuce

1 head radicchio

½ small red onion, thinly sliced

1 pint (300 g) heirloom cherry tomatoes, cut into quarters

1 (15-ounce/430 g) can chickpeas, rinsed and drained

8 ounces (225 g) fresh pearl mozzarella

4 ounces (115 g) provolone cheese, cut into medium dice

4 ounces (115 g) Genoa salami, cut into small cubes

5 pepperoncini (stems discarded), cut into thin slices

2 teaspoons chopped oregano for garnish

Combine all the ingredients for the vinaigrette in a small bowl and whisk to combine. Season with salt and pepper as needed.

Cut the iceberg lettuce in half through the core. Remove and discard the outer leaves and discard the core. Separate the lettuce leaves, stack 2 or 3 leaves on top of one another, then cut them lengthwise into ¼-inch-wide (6 mm) strips. Repeat with the remaining leaves. Thinly slice the radicchio in the same way.

In a large, wide bowl, combine the lettuce and radicchio, tomatoes, chickpeas, mozzarella, provolone, salami, and pepperoncini. Season with salt to taste and toss to thoroughly combine. Drizzle 6 tablespoons (90 ml) of the vinaigrette over the salad and toss gently to coat the salad evenly. Taste and add more vinaigrette as needed, plus salt and pepper. Transfer the salad to a large platter, sprinkle with extra oregano, and serve.

*Serves 4 as an entrée, 6 as a side dish*

# *Chicken*
# Taco Salad

*Do you remember those giant taco salads you would eat in middle and high school? The ones served up in an enormous fried tortilla shell and slathered with ranch dressing that you'd order because you thought they were cool and semi-healthy? I'm not going to say that it wasn't . . . but I've matured, and so should my salad. This updated version is equally as delicious but lighter, thanks to the omission of the fried shell and upgrading the dressing to my Cilantro Vinaigrette.*

Ingredients

For the chicken

2 teaspoons olive oil

1 small onion, diced

2 cloves garlic, chopped

1 pound (455 g) ground chicken

2 tablespoons taco seasoning

For the salad

3 heads baby romaine lettuce, thinly shredded

1 cup (145 g) cherry tomatoes, halved or quartered

½ cup (55 g) grated Cheddar cheese

2 ears of corn, shucked and corn kernels sliced off the cob

2 ripe avocados, pitted, peeled, and diced

3 scallions, sliced

Fresh cilantro leaves

A few tablespoons chopped or sliced red onion

1 cup (185 g) canned black beans, rinsed and drained

Cilantro Vinaigrette (page 254)

To make the chicken: Heat the olive oil in a medium skillet over medium-high heat. Add the onions and sauté for 5 minutes, or until they are soft. Add the garlic and sauté for 30 seconds more. Add the ground chicken and cook for 6 to 7 minutes, until fully cooked. Add the taco seasoning and ¼ cup (60 ml) water, or as needed, and reduce the heat to low. Simmer the mixture for 5 minutes while you assemble the salad.

To make the salad: To assemble this salad in one large serving bowl, layer half of the lettuce on the bottom of the bowl followed by half of all the other toppings. Add the second layer of lettuce on top and finish with the remaining toppings. Top with the chicken and toss the salad together with a few tablespoons of the vinaigrette. Add more vinaigrette as needed and serve immediately.

*Serves 4 to 6*

# Little Gem Salad
## with Avocado

*Any time I'm hosting a big party and going all out with the mains, this is my side salad of choice. It pairs with beef, chicken, pork, fish, pasta—you name it. And it works any time of year, and also any time of day—including breakfast, which I can personally attest to—it pretty much goes with everything. It's an all-around clutch salad that's there for you when you need it.*

**Ingredients**

3 to 4 heads Little Gem lettuce

2 ripe avocados, pitted, peeled, and sliced

1 bunch fresh chives, snipped

Lemon Vinaigrette (page 255)

Carefully trim the lettuce leaves off the head. Rinse well and dry. Toss the whole leaves, the avocado, and snipped chives with the lemon-shallot vinaigrette and serve on a large platter.

*Serves 4 to 6*

# Thai Beef Salad

*The dressing on this salad, with its bright, citrusy lemongrass and cilantro flavors, is reason enough to make it. Add to that beef that's been given a salty-savory marinade treatment, then tossed with crisp lettuce, chiles, and even more herbs, and you've got yourself a salad that will have everyone licking their plates clean.*

## Ingredients

### For the marinated beef

Juice of 1 lime

2 cloves garlic, minced

1 tablespoon honey

1 tablespoon fish sauce

¼ cup (60 ml) sesame oil

¼ cup (60 ml) soy sauce

1 to 1½ pounds (455 to 680 g) flank or strip steak, patted dry

### For the lemongrass-cilantro dressing

2 cloves garlic, minced

1 tablespoon minced fresh lemongrass

Juice of 1 lime, plus more for serving

1 tablespoon honey

¼ cup (60 ml) sesame oil

¼ cup (60 ml) olive oil

¼ cup (10 g) minced fresh cilantro

### For the crunchy peanut topping

1 tablespoon toasted sesame oil

2 tablespoons sesame seeds

3 tablespoons peanuts, chopped

Kosher salt

### For the salad

3 heads baby romaine, chopped

1 red pepper, seeded and julienned

3 Persian cucumbers, sliced on the bias

1 bunch scallions, sliced on the bias

1 cup (40 g) loosely packed fresh Thai basil leaves

1 cup (40 g) loosely packed fresh cilantro leaves

2 chiles (such as jalapeños or red chiles), seeded and sliced

½ red onion, sliced

**To marinate the beef:** In a large bowl, whisk together the lime juice, garlic, honey, fish sauce, sesame oil, and soy sauce. Submerge the steak in the marinade and flip to coat the meat. Cover and refrigerate for at least 2 hours or up to overnight.

**To make the salad dressing:** In a medium bowl, whisk together all the ingredients until well combined; set aside.

**To make the peanut topping:** Warm the toasted sesame oil in a small skillet over medium heat. Add the sesame seeds and peanuts and stir to coat in the oil. Cook until the peanuts and sesame seeds are toasted and fragrant, about 5 minutes. Season to taste with salt; set aside. Allow the steak to rest in the marinade at room temperature for 30 minutes before grilling.

**Meanwhile, make the salad:** Gather and prep all the salad ingredients and arrange them on a large serving platter. Drizzle with the dressing.

In a large cast-iron skillet or grill pan over high heat, warm 1 tablespoon of oil until almost smoking. Sear the steak on both sides until the internal temperature reaches 135°F (57°C). Transfer to a cutting board to rest for 10 minutes. Slice the steak thinly and top the salad. Sprinkle with the crunchy peanut topping and serve.

*Serves 4*

# Loaded Fattoush

*I've been making fattoush for years—partly because it's fun to say and partly because it's a great excuse to throw freshly crisped pita into a salad. Plus, there's nothing more delicious once you've drizzled the sumac dressing over the mix. And no, you can't sub out the sumac. It adds a unique brightness to the dish, so I strongly encourage you to seek it out at your local market, spice shop, or online. I promise you'll put it to good use once you have it in your pantry—if anything, to make this salad over and over again!*

## Ingredients

### For the fried pita

1 teaspoon ground sumac

1 teaspoon garlic powder

1 teaspoon kosher salt

¼ cup (60 ml) vegetable oil (or another high-smoke-point oil)

2 pita pockets, ripped into pieces

### For the salad

2 heads baby romaine lettuce

1 bunch Easter egg radishes, washed, trimmed, and quartered (roughly 10 radishes)

1 red bell pepper, sliced

4 scallions, thinly sliced

2 cups (190 g) heirloom cherry tomatoes, halved

3 Persian cucumbers, sliced

½ cup (25 g) fresh mint leaves

¼ cup (25 g) fresh parsley leaves

4 teaspoons ground sumac, soaked in 4 teaspoons warm water for 15 minutes

3 tablespoons fresh lemon juice

2 tablespoons pomegranate molasses

2 small cloves garlic, minced

2 teaspoons red wine vinegar

6 tablespoons (90 ml) olive oil

Kosher salt

**To make the fried pita:** Put the sumac, garlic powder, and salt in a small bowl and mix to combine.

Heat the vegetable oil in a nonstick skillet over medium-high heat. Add half of the ripped pitas to the oil and fry until crispy, 3 to 4 minutes, tossing every 30 seconds to ensure even frying. Remove the fried pita to a paper towel–lined plate to drain. Season with half of the sumac mixture. Repeat with the remaining pita until all the bread is fried and seasoned. Set aside to cool.

**To make the salad:** In a large bowl, arrange the lettuce, radishes, bell peppers, scallions, tomatoes, cucumber, mint, and parsley. In a smaller bowl, combine the sumac and its soaking water with the lemon juice, pomegranate molasses, garlic, vinegar, and olive oil. Whisk until well blended and season with salt as needed. Add the dressing to the salad and gently toss until lightly dressed. Sprinkle the top of the salad with the fried pita and serve immediately.

*Serves 4 to 6*

# Gaby's Ode to
# Zuni's Roast Chicken
## with Bread Salad

*Zuni Café in San Francisco is one of the most celebrated restaurants in the country, and their chicken salad is one for the record books. But instead of telling you to book a trip to SF just to eat this salad (which would not be a bad call, just sayin'), I'm giving you my interpretation of it. Do yourself a favor and make this salad, and serve it with a side of fries and an Aperol spritz (page 138). FYI: The dry brine for the chicken starts 24 to 48 hours ahead of serving, so mentally prepare yourself for a project! It's all about drying out the skin so you get the most delicious, crispy skin of all time! It's 100 percent worth it.*

---

### Ingredients

#### For the chicken

1 (4- to 5-pound/1.8 to 2.3 kg) chicken, giblets removed

3 tablespoons kosher salt

¼ teaspoon freshly cracked black pepper

2 tablespoons minced mixed fresh herbs (such as thyme, rosemary, and sage)

2 tablespoons extra-virgin olive oil

#### For the bread salad

1 (8- to 10-ounce/225 to 280 g) round loaf country-style white bread (not sourdough)

6 tablespoons (90 ml) extra-virgin olive oil

5 cloves garlic, thinly sliced

6 scallions, thinly sliced, including part of the dark green stalks

2 tablespoons dried currants

2 tablespoons red wine vinegar

2 tablespoons hot water

2 tablespoons champagne vinegar

Kosher salt and freshly cracked black pepper

3 cups (90 g) loosely packed peppery lettuce, preferably mâche

¼ cup (35 g) pine nuts, toasted

**Make the chicken:** Pat the chicken all over with paper towels to make sure it's very dry. Use your fingers to loosen the skin on the breast, making a pocket that you'll use to place the chopped herbs in. Place the chicken on a rack in a roasting pan and sprinkle liberally with the salt, making sure to get the bottom, inside cav- ity and the wings. Tuck the wings behind the breast and tie the legs with butcher's twine. Lightly sprinkle with the pepper. Place the chicken, uncovered, in the refrigerator for 24 to 48 hours to slowly dehydrate the skin.

Continued

After the chicken has air dried, remove it from the refrigerator and let it sit at room temperature for about 30 minutes. Meanwhile, preheat the oven to 425°F (220°C).

Tuck the herbs into the pocket that you created, drizzle the chicken with the olive oil, and roast for 1 hour 15 minutes, rotating the bird halfway through cooking to ensure even browning. Once done, a meat thermometer inserted into the thickest part of the thigh should register at 165°F (74°C) and the juices should run clean. Let rest under a foil tent for 10 to 15 minutes before carving.

Meanwhile, make the bread salad: Set the oven to broil and adjust a rack 4 to 6 inches (10 to 15 cm) from the broiler.

Remove the crust from the loaf of bread and tear the bread into large chunks ranging in size from 2 to 3 inches (5 to 7.5 cm) and other small crumbs (about 4 cups/180 g in all). Place on a baking sheet and drizzle the bread with 2 tablespoons of the olive oil. Broil the bread until toasted, turning the pieces with tongs every few minutes. This happens quickly; some dark spots are fine, but keep your eyes on the bread to prevent burning. Transfer the toasted bread into a large oven-safe serving dish.

In a small skillet over medium-low heat, sauté the garlic and scallions with 2 tablespoons of the olive oil for 2 to 3 minutes, until fragrant, and then pour the oil over the toasted bread.

Combine the dried currants with the red wine vinegar mixed with the hot water. Let sit for 10 minutes before draining and tossing with the toasted bread.

Mix together the champagne vinegar with the remaining 2 tablespoons olive oil and toss with the bread salad in the serving dish. Season with salt and pepper.

When ready to serve, toss a few handfuls of lettuce and the pine nuts into the bread salad. Serve the chicken pieces on top of the salad, letting the juices from the chicken season the salad.

*Serves 6*

# Baby Kale, Goat Cheese, Candied Walnuts &
# Lentil Salad

*When I was growing up, my mom made lentil burgers on the regular. And not only that, she'd make like two dozen and freeze them for meals during the week. I wouldn't always be so pumped about that because I was a picky kid and thought lentils were weird (nothing a ton of ketchup couldn't fix). But fast-forward to now and . . . sorry Mom, I was wrong. In addition to being loaded with all sorts of nutrients, lentils are hearty and versatile, pairing with just about any flavors you put them with. Goat cheese and candied walnuts? Why not!*

---

## Ingredients

1 large sweet potato, cut into ½-inch (12 mm) dice (about 2 cups/170 g)

3 tablespoons extra-virgin olive oil

Kosher salt and freshly cracked black pepper

1 cup (190 g) green lentils

1 bag (5 ounces/140 g) baby kale

½ bag (2½ ounces/70 g) baby arugula or other bitter greens

Lemon Tahini Dressing (page 252)

4 ounces (115 g) goat cheese, chilled and crumbled

½ cup (50 g) candied walnuts, roughly chopped

½ red onion, thinly sliced

½ bunch scallions, sliced on the bias

½ cup (25 g) fresh mint leaves

Preheat the oven to 400°F (205°C). In a medium bowl, toss the sweet potatoes with the olive oil. Season generously with salt and pepper. Spread the sweet potatoes into an even layer on a baking sheet and roast until lightly browned and tender, 15 to 20 minutes. Meanwhile, cook the lentils according to package instructions. Let cool.

To prepare the salad, put the kale and arugula in a large bowl. Add ½ cup (120 ml) of the dressing and toss to coat. Top with the roasted sweet potatoes, lentils, goat cheese, walnuts, red onion, scallions, and mint. Drizzle with the remaining dressing and serve.

*Serves 4 as an entrée, 6 as an appetizer*

# Black Bean Soup

*I have such fond childhood memories of my mom making this for us . . .
and then letting us pile on an insane amount of cheese. (We were seriously
aggressive.) For this version, I've swapped all that cheese for sour cream,
which gives the soup the perfect amount of tangy creaminess. It's easy to
make, fantastic as leftovers, and freezes well too.*

### Ingredients

2 tablespoons olive oil, plus more for
serving

1 onion, diced

2 carrots, peeled and diced

1 stalk celery, diced

3 cloves garlic, minced

1½ tablespoons ground cumin

1 to 2 tablespoons adobo sauce from a
can of chipotles in adobo, depending
on desired spiciness

Kosher salt and freshly cracked pepper

4 (15-ounce/430 g) cans black beans,
drained and rinsed

2½ cups (600 ml) vegetable broth

Juice of 1 lime, plus more limes cut into
wedges for serving

½ cup (120 ml) sour cream

1 ripe avocado, pitted, peeled, and diced

Fresh cilantro sprigs

Fresh scallions, thinly sliced

Warm the olive oil in a large pot over medium heat. Add the onion, carrots, and celery and cook until softened, about 10 minutes. Add the garlic and cook for an additional minute. Stir in the cumin and adobo sauce and cook until the vegetables are well coated and very fragrant, about 5 minutes. Season with salt and pepper. Add the beans and vegetable broth and bring to a boil over medium-high heat. Reduce the heat to low and cook, covered, until the beans are very tender, about 30 minutes.

Transfer half the soup into a blender and blend until smooth. Return the puree to the pot and stir to combine. Taste and adjust the seasoning with salt, pepper, and the juice of 1 lime. Divide the soup among bowls. Top with a drizzle of olive oil and some sour cream, avocado, cilantro, and scallions. Serve lime wedges alongside.

*Serves 8*

# Emily's Chicken & White Bean
# Chili Verde

*Emily, one of my very best friends in the entire world, has had a HUGE impact on my life ever since we met on the tennis court back when we were nine years old. She taught me to drive, she basically doubles as my therapist when needed, is the big sister I never had, plus many more things that I can't even fit on this page. She introduced me to this white bean chili, which is EXACTLY what I want in a stew. It's flavorful, chunky, great as leftovers, and just like Emily, I love it to the end of the Earth and back.*

## Ingredients

1½ pounds (680 g) tomatillos, husked and halved

3 poblano chiles, halved

2 Anaheim chiles, halved

1 jalapeño chile, halved

6 cloves garlic, skin still on

1 bunch fresh cilantro, stems removed

Juice of 1 lime

2 teaspoons ground cumin

Kosher salt and freshly cracked black pepper

2 cups (480 ml) chicken broth

1½ pounds (680 g) boneless, skinless chicken thighs

2 tablespoons olive oil

1 yellow onion, thinly sliced

1 (15-ounce/430 g) can white beans

### For serving

Tortilla chips

Scallions, thinly sliced

Radishes, thinly sliced

Fresh cilantro sprigs

Freshly grated Monterey Jack cheese

Preheat the broiler and line a large baking sheet with aluminum foil. Place the tomatillos and all of the chile peppers cut side down on the pan along with the unpeeled garlic cloves. Broil for 10 minutes, or until the tomatillos are soft and the peppers are charred.

Transfer the chiles to a glass bowl and seal with plastic wrap to steam (leave the tomatillos and garlic on the baking sheet for now). After steaming for 10 minutes, remove and discard the skin from the peppers. Peel the garlic.

In a blender, combine the tomatillos, garlic, assorted roasted and peeled peppers, cilantro, lime juice, cumin, salt and pepper to taste, and the chicken broth. Blend the ingredients until smooth and set aside.

Season the chicken thighs liberally with kosher salt and freshly cracked black pepper.

In a large heavy-bottom skillet or Dutch oven, heat the olive oil over medium-high heat. Add the chicken thighs and sear both sides until golden brown. Add the onions and sauté for a few minutes before adding the tomatillo mixture from the blender. Bring to a boil, reduce the heat to medium, cover, and simmer for 20 to 30 minutes, until the chicken is cooked through, then add the beans and continue to cook until they are warmed. Remove the chicken to a cutting board and shred the chicken with a fork. Add the chicken back into the mixture. Taste and adjust the salt and pepper as needed. Serve in bowls with tortilla chips on the side and tons of the garnishes on top.

*Serves 6*

## Chapter 4
# Soul Mate: Carbs

I'll never say no to carbs. Pizza and pasta (aka Hard Carbs) are my love language, and I'm pretty sure I was meant to live in Italy (aka Carb Capital) at some point in my life. So you won't be surprised to hear that I don't believe in cutting out carbs, even if you're on the "wellness" trip. I think that—like everything in life—moderation is key. Plus, we need carbs to survive (hello, brain food!), so we might as well enjoy every single delicious bite.

# Lemon Broccoli
# Pesto Pasta

*I can vividly remember the six or so dinners that we'd have on a rotating basis while I was growing up, and broccoli pesto pasta was one of them. I was always SO pumped on those nights because I was getting my fav veggie with a heaping helping of cheese and carbs. It's a recipe for success, if you ask me!*

## Ingredients

Kosher salt

1 large head of broccoli, stems and florets roughly chopped

6 tablespoons (55 g) pine nuts, lightly toasted

3 cups (300 g) grated Parmesan cheese

2 cups (80 g) packed fresh basil leaves, plus more for garnish

Zest and juice of 2 lemons, plus more for serving

1 cup (240 ml) extra-virgin olive oil

Freshly cracked black pepper

1 pound (455 g) short pasta

Bring a large pot of water to a boil. Salt generously, then add the broccoli and cook until crisp tender, about 4 minutes. Use a slotted spoon to transfer to a large bowl of ice water. Do not discard the cooking water. Drain the broccoli and dry well on paper towels. In the bowl of a food processor, combine the broccoli stems and florets, 4 tablespoons (35 g) of the pine nuts, 1½ cups (150 g) of the Parmesan, the basil leaves, and lemon zest and juice. Process until combined, about 30 seconds. Scrape down the sides of the bowl. While the processor is running, slowly stream in the olive oil. Season with salt and pepper to taste.

Bring the same pot of water back to a boil. Add the pasta and cook according to package instructions. Drain the pasta, reserving ¼ cup (60 ml) pasta water, and return the pot over medium-low heat. Add 1 cup (100 g) of the Parmesan cheese and the pasta water and cook, stirring constantly, until the cheese coats the pasta, about 1 minute. Remove from the heat and add half of the broccoli pesto. Transfer to a large serving bowl. Top with the remaining ½ cup (50 g) Parmesan, 2 tablespoons pine nuts, and lemon zest. Garnish with basil. Reserve extra broccoli pesto or freeze for another use.

*Serves 4 to 6*

# *Chipotle Chorizo*
# Mac 'n' Cheese

*Mac with two kinds of cheese and crumbled chorizo plus a bread crumb topping—you say over the top, I say just enough.*

---

### Ingredients

4 cups (960 ml) whole milk

½ cup (115 g/1 stick) unsalted butter

½ cup (65 g) all-purpose flour

1 pound (455 g) large elbow macaroni

6 ounces (170 g) pork or soy chorizo

1 teaspoon kosher salt

½ teaspoon freshly cracked black pepper

3 chipotles in adobo, diced

8 ounces (225 g) shredded pepper Jack cheese

4 ounces (115 g) shredded Gouda cheese, plus ¼ cup (30 g) for topping

1 cup (80 g) panko bread crumbs

1 tablespoon unsalted butter, melted

Preheat the oven to 350°F (175°C). Spray a 9 by 13-inch (23 by 33 cm) baking dish with cooking spray and set aside.

In a medium saucepan over medium heat, simmer the milk until it almost comes to a boil; remove from the heat and set aside.

In a large saucepan, melt the butter over medium heat. Whisk in the flour and continue to whisk until the butter and flour mixture is a pale blond color, 3 to 4 minutes.

Quickly pour the warmed milk into the flour mixture, whisking constantly until well combined. Continue to whisk the sauce until it's thick and can coat the back of a spoon, about 3 minutes. Remove from the heat and set aside.

In a large pot of boiling salted water, cook the pasta to al dente, about 2 minutes less than recommended cooking time. Drain the pasta and run under cold water to stop the cooking. The pasta will continue to cook in the sauce.

Remove the chorizo from its casing. Cook the chorizo in a small skillet over medium-high heat until slightly dry and browned, 6 to 8 minutes. Transfer to a paper towel–lined plate to drain away excess fat. Set aside.

Place the sauce back over medium-high heat and stir until warm. Season with the salt, pepper, and chipotles and stir to combine. Add the pepper Jack and 4 ounces (115 g) of the Gouda in handfuls and stir to melt into the sauce. Add the pasta to the sauce and and fold in the chorizo, then pour the mixture into the prepared baking dish.

Combine the panko and melted butter in a bowl, stirring to mix. Top the macaroni with the remaining ¼ cup (30 g) shredded Gouda and sprinkle with the panko topping. Bake for 15 to 20 minutes, until bubbling.

*Serves 6 to 8*

# *White Wine Chili Flake*
# Pasta

*I would tell you that you should use your leftover white wine to make this, but really, what is leftover wine? Is that even a thing? Didn't think so. Here's what you do: Buy a bottle of wine, pour yourself a glass, make this recipe, then invite friends over to finish the bottle. Or maybe have them pick up one or two more bottles on their way over. This pasta is so deeply flavorful yet easy to make that you're going to want it as part of your weekly dinner rotation. Added bonus: The garlic and white wine simmering together will make your house smell like Italy.*

---

### Ingredients

3 tablespoons unsalted butter

3 tablespoons olive oil

1 teaspoon red pepper flakes

1 pound (455 g) small yellow cherry tomatoes

8 cloves garlic, finely minced

1 cup (240 ml) white wine

Kosher salt and freshly cracked black pepper

Zest and juice of 2 lemons

¼ cup (13 g) finely chopped fresh parsley

10 ounces (280 g) malfadini or linguini

1 cup (100 g) toasted Homemade Chunky Garlic Bread Crumbs (page 256)

In a large skillet, melt the butter in the olive oil. Add the red pepper flakes and tomatoes and sauté until the tomatoes start to burst. Add the garlic and sauté until fragrant, about 30 seconds. Add the wine, a pinch of salt, and plenty of black pepper, and bring to a simmer. Let the wine cook down for 2 to 5 minutes.

Add the lemon zest and season with salt and pepper. Sauté for 1 minute to release the flavor. Stir in the parsley and half the lemon juice, or more as needed. Toss to combine.

Cook the pasta according to the package directions. Drain and toss the pasta with the sauce and season with salt and pepper as needed. Toss with the bread crumbs. Serve immediately.

*Serves 4*

# *Pink* Cacio e Pepe

*There's a restaurant in Brooklyn called Lilia, and I make a point of visiting every time I'm in New York. Before I ever went, everyone told me that the pink peppercorn pasta would change my life. And you know what? They weren't kidding. It's a classic, creamy cacio e pepe but with the addition of pink peppercorns instead of the traditional black, which add their own unique heat, floral flavor, and pretty pink color. (Though you could use black peppercorns instead.) Now I have to make this on a weekly basis because there's no way I'd ever be able to get to Brooklyn every time I craved this dish.*

---

### Ingredients

Kosher salt

10 ounces (280 g) spaghetti

3 tablespoons unsalted butter, cut into cubes

2 to 3 teaspoons freshly cracked pink peppercorns

¾ cup (70 g) finely grated Parmesan cheese

⅓ cup (30 g) finely grated Pecorino cheese

Bring a large pot of water to a boil and salt it. Once boiling, add the spaghetti and cook, stirring occasionally, until al dente. Drain, reserving ¾ cup (180 ml) pasta cooking water.

Meanwhile, melt 2 tablespoons of the butter in a large skillet over medium heat. Add the cracked pink pepper and cook, swirling the pan, until toasted, about 1 minute.

Add ½ cup (120 ml) of the reserved pasta water to the skillet and bring to a simmer. Add the spaghetti and remaining 1 tablespoon butter. Reduce the heat to low and add the Parmesan, stirring and tossing the pasta with tongs until the cheese is melted. Remove the pan from the heat; add the Pecorino, stirring and tossing until the cheese melts and the sauce coats the pasta. (Add more pasta water if the sauce seems dry.) Serve immediately.

*Serves 4*

# Goat Cheese Polenta
## with Cherry Tomatoes & Basil Vinaigrette

*About a year or two ago, I had an epiphany: I needed to make more polenta, especially when I was having people over. It's so easy to make, and it takes on the flavor of whatever you fold in or sprinkle on top. So then and there I decided to add a recipe to my repertoire that highlights polenta along with three of my all-time favorite ingredients: goat cheese, cherry tomatoes, and basil vinaigrette. And when tomato season is over, I sub in Caramelized Mushrooms (page 115) for the tomatoes to keep the party goin' all year long.*

---

### Ingredients

2 pints (600 g) cherry tomatoes

¼ cup (60 ml) olive oil

Kosher salt and freshly cracked black pepper

3 cups (840 ml) whole milk, plus more as needed

1 cup (180 g) semolina flour

¼ cup (55 g) unsalted butter, cut into chunks

8 ounces (225 g) goat cheese

Basil Vinaigrette (page 254)

Fresh basil

Preheat the oven to 400°F (205°C). Toss the tomatoes with the olive oil and season with salt and pepper. Spread into an even layer on a baking sheet and roast the tomatoes until just blistered and beginning to burst, about 25 minutes.

Meanwhile, in a large saucepan over medium heat, bring the milk to a simmer. Slowly whisk in the semolina flour. Continue whisking until thickened, about 2 minutes. If too thick, continue to add milk until you reach desired consistency. Remove from the heat and stir in the butter until melted, then add half of the goat cheese. Season to taste with salt and pepper. Transfer the polenta to a serving bowl. Top with the blistered tomatoes, remaining goat cheese, and basil vinaigrette. Garnish with fresh basil.

*Serves 4 to 6*

# *Garlic Kale*
# Pizza

*This pie is my kind of balance—all the chewy dough, all the Parm and mozzarella, and all the garlicky kale. If you're not into kale, the answer is yes, you can sub in spinach!*

---

### Ingredients

5 tablespoons (75 ml) olive oil

4 cloves garlic, minced

1 shallot, sliced

2 Fresno chile peppers, halved, seeded, and thinly sliced

6 ounces (170 g) baby kale, plus a few extra leaves for garnish

Kosher salt and freshly cracked black pepper

1 pound (455 g) pizza dough

Cornmeal or flour for pizza peel (optional)

8 cloves garlic, finely chopped

2 cups (220 g) torn fresh mozzarella cheese

½ cup (50 g) shredded Parmesan cheese

Red pepper flakes

Lemon wedges

In a large skillet, heat 3 tablespoons of the olive oil over medium heat. Add the minced garlic, shallot, and Fresno chiles and cook for about 1 minute, until fragrant. Add the kale and stir until wilted, 3 to 5 minutes. Remove from the heat. Season with salt and pepper and set aside.

Preheat the oven to 500°F (260°C). About 30 minutes before cooking the pizza, put your pizza stone in the oven.

Divide the dough in half. Stretch each half of the dough in a circular motion, then lay out the disks on a flat surface and further flatten them out using a rolling pin. If you have a pizza peel, sprinkle some cornmeal or flour on it and place one of the stretched-out doughs on the peel.

Once your pizza dough is flat and ready to be cooked, brush the remaining 2 tablespoons olive oil over the pizzas and sprinkle them with the finely chopped garlic. Pile with the torn mozzarella and the Parmesan and top with the wilted kale. Season with salt and pepper and red pepper flakes.

Transfer the pizza into the oven and bake until the crust is golden, 8 to 12 minutes. Remove from the oven, slice, and serve with lemon wedges.

*Serves 4 to 6*

# Modern-Day Margherita Pizza

*My mama is a little bit of a picky eater. When we go out for pizza, I'll order something with mushrooms, my dad almost always gets something with meat, for Thomas it's sausage, my sister is a wild card, and my mom without fail will get the simplest of simple: the margherita. But I'd never knock such a straightforward pie—it's a tried-and-true favorite, plus I'll always eat whatever she doesn't finish. And because there are four pizzas in this book, I wanted to dedicate one to her. I opted for a tomato confit instead of the traditional sliced tomatoes and basil vinaigrette instead of fresh basil (you know it's just gonna wilt on the pizza), and it's pure, simple perfection.*

---

### Ingredients

1 pound (455 g) cherry tomatoes, halved

⅓ cup (75 ml) good quality olive oil

6 cloves garlic, peeled

Kosher salt and freshly cracked black pepper

1 pound (455 g) pizza dough

Cornmeal or flour for pizza peel (optional)

8 ounces (225 g) fresh mozzarella cheese, torn into ½-inch (12 mm) pieces

½ cup (120 ml) Basil Vinaigrette (page 254)

Red pepper flakes

In a medium skillet over medium-high heat, combine the tomatoes and olive oil. Add the garlic and a pinch of salt and pepper. Once the oil starts to heat up and the tomatoes start to blister, reduce the heat to medium-low and let the tomatoes simmer for at least 30 minutes or up to 1 hour, stirring every 10 minutes. The tomatoes should be falling apart. Remove the pan from the heat and allow the confit to cool for at least 20 minutes. Makes approximately 1½ cups (250 g).

Preheat the oven to 500°F (260°C). About 30 minutes before cooking the pizza, put your pizza stone in the oven.

Divide the dough in half. Stretch each half of the dough in a circular motion, then lay out the disks on a flat surface and further flatten them out using a rolling pin. If you have a pizza peel, sprinkle some flour or cornmeal on it and place one of the stretched-out doughs on the peel.

Once your pizza dough is flat and ready to be cooked, spread ½ cup (125 g) of the garlic tomato confit on each pizza. Top with the mozzarella. Transfer the pizzas to the oven and bake until the crust is golden, 8 to 12 minutes.

Remove the pizzas from the oven. Drizzle with the basil vinaigrette, season with salt, pepper, and red pepper flakes, and serve immediately.

*Serves 4 to 6*

# *Burrata Panzanella* Pizza

*Panzanella pizza you ask? YES. Prepare to have your life changed. Let's start at the bottom: First, we've got crust smothered with my garlic Parm sauce. Then, after that's baked, we add burrata, lightly dressed arugula, and . . . wait for it . . . bread crumbs. How did I not think of this sooner?! When you take a bite, it's the perfect combination of flavors and textures that you never knew you needed . . . but you really, really do.*

---

### Ingredients

⅓ cup (75 ml) olive oil

⅓ cup (30 g) shredded Parmesan cheese

6 cloves garlic, minced

1 teaspoon red pepper flakes, plus more for serving

Kosher salt and freshly cracked black pepper

1 pound (455 g) pizza dough

Cornmeal or flour for pizza peel (optional)

8 ounces (225 g) burrata cheese

1 to 2 cups (20 to 40 g) baby arugula

3 tablespoons Lemon Vinaigrette (page 255)

½ cup (50 g) Homemade Chunky Garlic Bread Crumbs (page 256)

In a medium bowl, combine the oil, Parmesan, garlic, 1 teaspoon red pepper flakes, and salt and black pepper. Set aside.

Preheat the oven to 500°F (260°C). About 30 minutes before cooking the pizza, put your pizza stone in the oven.

Divide the dough in half. Stretch each half of the dough in a circular motion, then lay out the disks on a flat surface and flatten them out using a rolling pin. If you have a pizza peel, sprinkle some cornmeal or flour on it and place one of the stretched-out doughs on the peel. Once your pizza dough is flat and ready to be cooked, brush half of the garlic–Parmesan sauce over each pizza. Transfer the pizzas to the oven and bake until the crust is golden, 8 to 12 minutes.

Remove the pizza from the oven. Tear the burrata into pieces and evenly distribute the cheese on top of each pizza. Toss the arugula with the vinaigrette and top each pizza. Sprinkle with the bread crumbs and more red pepper flakes and serve.

*Serves 4 to 6*

# Caramelized Onion & Mushroom Pizza

*Mushrooms are my go-to choice for pizza toppings, and I'm always reaching for them for other recipes too, especially when combining their deep earthiness with rich, sweet caramelized onions. So when I wanted to give my usual pizza sitch an upgrade, I immediately thought of that combination. The key to these flavors playing well together is a spritz of fresh lemon juice, which adds much-needed brightness and makes the whole thing that much tastier. Note: Take your time when making the caramelized veggies—they really shouldn't be rushed!*

---

### Ingredients

1 pound (455 g) pizza dough

2 tablespoons olive oil

6 cloves garlic, finely chopped

1 cup (110 g) shredded mozzarella cheese

1 cup (110 g) shredded Fontina cheese

1 cup (130 g) Caramelized Mushrooms (recipe follows)

1 cup (about 195 g) Caramelized Onions (recipe follows)

Fresh thyme leaves

Maldon sea salt and freshly cracked black pepper

1 lemon

Preheat the oven to 450°F (230°C).

Divide the dough into 2 equal pieces. On a lightly floured surface roll each piece of dough into a thin circle. Transfer to an oiled baking sheet and drizzle with equal amounts of the olive oil, garlic, mozzarella, Fontina, and caramelized mushrooms and onions. Bake for 12 to 14 minutes, until the cheese is bubbly and golden brown around the edges.

Remove from the oven, top with fresh thyme, and season with salt and pepper. Serve immediately with a squeeze of lemon.

*Serves 4 to 6*

---

## Caramelized Mushrooms

3 tablespoons olive oil

1 pound (455 g) wild mushrooms, trimmed

4 large cloves garlic, chopped

½ teaspoon kosher salt

¼ teaspoon freshly cracked black pepper

Heat a large heavy skillet over medium-high heat until hot. Add the olive oil, then add the mushrooms and sauté, stirring frequently, until golden brown, about 15 to 20 minutes. About 1 minute before the mushrooms are done, add the garlic and stir to combine. Season with salt and pepper and set aside.

## Caramelized Onions

2 tablespoons olive oil

2 yellow onions, finely diced

Kosher salt

In a large skillet, heat the olive oil over medium-high heat. Add the onion and sauté for 10 to 15 minutes until it starts to caramelize. Reduce the heat to medium and add a few tablespoons of water starting at the 15-minute mark and continue to caramelize for a total of 45 minutes, until the onions are deeply brown but not burnt. Season with salt to taste and set aside.

# *French Onion*
# Grilled Cheese

*We all love a French onion soup, right? But can we also all agree that the best parts are the cheesy toast and the onions? This grilled cheese takes the high-lights of this classic dish, sans broth—so more cheese and bread, and less splat-tering all over your clothes. Everybody wins.*

## Ingredients

2 tablespoons olive oil

2 yellow onions, thinly sliced

2 sprigs fresh thyme

¼ cup (60 ml) red wine

Kosher salt

4 slices bread

4 ounces (115 g) thinly sliced Gruyère cheese

2 teaspoons grated Parmesan cheese

2 tablespoons unsalted butter

In a large skillet, heat the olive oil over medium-high heat. Add the onions and thyme and sauté for 10 to 15 minutes, until the onions start to caramelize. Reduce the heat to medium, add a few tablespoons of water if the onions start to stick, and continue to caramelize for 25 to 30 minutes, until golden brown. Pour in the wine with 5 minutes to go and let the alcohol and liquid cook out. Season with salt, remove the thyme sprigs, and transfer the caramelized onions to a medium bowl. Wipe out the skillet, or wash it, if needed.

Lay out 2 slices of bread on a clean flat surface. Place 1 ounce (30 g) of the Gruyère on one piece of bread, followed by about ⅓ cup (about 65 g) of the caramelized onions, 1 teaspoon of Parmesan cheese, and then another ounce (30 g) of the Gruyère. Top with the remaining slice of bread, and press down gently. Repeat the process for the other sandwich.

In the cleaned skillet, melt 1 tablespoon of the butter over medium heat. Add the sandwiches and cook until the bottoms turn golden brown, 3 to 4 minutes. Reduce the heat to low if they brown too quickly. Add the remaining 1 tablespoon butter, flip the sandwiches, press down with the flat side of a spatula, and cook until the cheese has fully melted and the bottoms turn golden brown, 3 to 4 minutes. If you need to melt the cheese a bit more, cover the skillet with a lid and turn off the heat. Slice the sandwiches in half and serve immediately.

*Serves 2*

# *Bacon, Cheddar & Tomato*
# Grilled Cheese

*My dad specializes in epic grilled cheese sandwiches, and I'm one lucky girl because he makes one for me every time I'm home. Depending on what's in the kitchen, it could be just good ol' Colby Jack cheese, or if the fridge is stocked and he's feelin' jazzy, it's bacon and Cheddar. For my version, I throw in a tomato confit for dipping, but it still tastes like home.*

---

## Ingredients
4 slices bread

6 ounces (170 g) thinly sliced sharp Cheddar cheese

4 slices applewood smoked bacon, cooked and torn into pieces

6 tablespoons (90 g) Garlic Tomato Confit (page 251), plus more for serving

4 tablespoons (55 g) unsalted butter

Lay out 2 slices of bread on a clean flat surface. Place one-fourth of the Cheddar on 1 piece of bread followed by half of the bacon and half of the tomato confit. Add another one-fourth of Cheddar on top. Top with the remaining slice of bread, and press down gently. Repeat the process for the other sandwich.

In a large skillet, melt 2 tablespoons of the butter over medium heat. Add the sandwiches and cook until the bottoms turn golden brown, 3 to 4 minutes. Reduce the heat to low if they brown too quickly. Add the remaining 2 tablespoons butter to the pan, flip the sandwiches, press down with the flat side of a spatula, and cook until the cheese has fully melted and the bottoms turn golden brown, 3 to 4 minutes. If you need to melt the cheese a bit more, cover the skillet with a lid and turn off the heat. Slice the sandwiches in half and serve immediately with extra tomato confit on the side.

*Serves 2*

# Salmon & Smashed Avocado Burger

*A few summers back, my family and I went on what was essentially an Alaskan safari. We took a boat to explore the Inside Passage, taking day trips to the shore to go hiking or heading out on smaller boats to go whale watching. To sum it up in a sentence: It was magical. Meanwhile, every day while we were off on an adventure, the ship would get deliveries from local fisherman with the freshest, most delicious salmon I've ever eaten in my life. One night they served a salmon burger, and I've pretty much been obsessed ever since. The only thing left to do was figure out how to make my own, complete with all the herbs, avocado, and pickled onions.*

---

## Ingredients

### For the cilantro aioli

1 clove garlic, finely minced

¼ cup (60 ml) mayonnaise

4 teaspoons Cilantro Vinaigrette (page 254)

### For the salmon patties

2 pounds (910 g) salmon, skinned and deboned

1 cup (100 g) super thinly sliced scallions

2 tablespoons finely chopped fresh chives

¼ cup (10 g) finely chopped fresh cilantro

¼ cup (13 g) finely chopped fresh parsley

½ jalapeño chile, finely chopped

2 large eggs

1 tablespoon olive oil

1 teaspoon kosher salt

1 cup (80 g) panko bread crumbs

6 brioche buns, buttered and toasted

2 large ripe avocados, pitted, peeled, and smashed and seasoned with salt, pepper, and lemon juice

Pickled Onions (page 256)

To make the aioli: In a small bowl, mix together the garlic, mayo, and cilantro vinaigrette. Taste and adjust the seasoning as needed. Set aside.

To make the salmon patties: Preheat an indoor grill pan over medium heat.

Using a large sharp knife, finely dice the salmon. Place the salmon in a large bowl; add the scallions, chives, cilantro, parsley, jalapeño, eggs, olive oil, and salt, and mix to combine.

Gently mix the panko bread crumbs into the salmon mixture and form 6 patties. Grill the patties for about 4 minutes on each side.

Place a spoonful of the aioli on the bottom of a buttered bun followed by a salmon patty. Top with a giant spoonful of the smashed avocado mixture and some pickled onions. Top with the other half of the bun. Repeat to assemble the rest of the burgers and enjoy immediately.

*Serves 6*

# Cape Cod Herb-Butter Seafood Rolls

*While spending some time on the East Coast last year, my love for lobster rolls and seafood boils was REAL. And it still is. So naturally, I combined these two things into one incredible roll. I know it's a divisive subject, so let's just get it out of the way up front: There's mayo and butter. As one of my favorite humans Belle English would say . . . Why choose when you can have both?*

## Ingredients

Kosher salt

3 (1-pound/455 g) live lobsters

1 pound (455 g) shrimp, peeled and deveined

¾ cup (170 g/1½ sticks) unsalted butter

¼ cup (13 g) chopped fresh parsley

2 tablespoons chopped fresh chives

1 tablespoon chopped fresh tarragon

3 tablespoons fresh lemon juice

2 teaspoons celery salt

Freshly cracked black pepper

6 brioche hot dog buns

2 tablespoons unsalted butter, at room temperature

¼ cup (60 ml) mayonnaise

Pour water into a large pot to a depth of 2 inches (5 cm). Salt it generously and bring to a rolling boil. Add the lobsters, cover the pot, and cook until the lobsters are bright red, about 9 minutes. In the last 2 minutes of cooking, add the shrimp and cook until opaque. Remove the lobsters and shrimp from the water and allow to cool. Then, carefully crack the lobster shells, pick the meat from the tail and claws, and cut it into approximately 2-inch (5 cm) pieces. Remove the tails from the shrimp and cut the shrimp in half. Transfer the lobster and shrimp to a large bowl. Set aside while you make herb butter.

In a large skillet over medium heat, melt the butter. Remove from heat and stir in the parsley, chives, and tarragon. Then add the lemon juice and celery salt and season to taste with salt and pepper. Pour the herb butter over the lobster and shrimp and toss to coat.

Heat a large skillet over medium heat. Spread the outside of the buns with butter and cook them until golden brown, about 2 minutes per side. Spread mayonnaise on the inside of the buns, then fill them with the lobster and shrimp mixture. Finish with a generous crack of black pepper.

*Makes 6 rolls*

# Kale & Leek Crostata

*Call it a crostata. Call it a tart. Call it a galette—no matter what you call it, this savory tart-like situation stuffed with kale, onions, garlic, and cheese is insanely delicious. Make it for breakfast, brunch, lunch, or dinner. Bring it to a party to share!*

---

### Ingredients

**For the dough**

1½ cups (190 g) all-purpose flour

½ cup (50 g) grated Parmesan cheese

1 teaspoon kosher salt

10 grinds freshly cracked black pepper

½ cup (115 g/1 stick) unsalted butter, cut into ¼-inch (6 mm) pieces

4 to 6 tablespoons (60 to 90 ml) ice cold water

**For the filling**

¼ cup (60 ml) olive oil

½ cup (115 g/1 stick) unsalted butter

1 onion, sliced

2 leeks, halved and sliced (about 3½ cups/315 g)

2 bunches kale, stripped and chopped (about 8 cups/520 g)

3 cloves garlic, minced

Kosher salt and freshly cracked black pepper

¼ cup (30 g) all-purpose flour

2 cups (480 ml) milk

1¼ cups (125 g) grated Parmesan cheese

1 cup (110 g) grated Gruyère cheese

1 large egg, lightly beaten

1 lemon

To make the dough: In a food processor, combine the flour, Parmesan, salt, and pepper. Add the butter and pulse until the mixture resembles a coarse cornmeal, about 10 pulses. Sprinkle with ¼ cup (60 ml) water and pulse until the dough is crumbly but holds together when squeezed, adding additional water if the dough is too dry. Turn the dough out onto a lightly floured surface. Form into a disk and wrap in plastic. Refrigerate at least 1 hour or up to 3 days.

To make the filling: In a large skillet over medium heat, warm the oil and 4 tablespoons (55 g) of the butter until the butter is melted. Add the onions and leeks and cook, stirring occasionally, until caramelized, about 15 minutes. Add the kale and garlic and cook until the kale is wilted and dark green, about 7 minutes more. Season the mixture with salt and pepper to taste; set aside.

In a large saucepan over medium heat, melt the remaining 4 tablespoons (55 g) of butter. Sprinkle in the flour and cook, whisking constantly until a thick paste forms, about 1 minute. Slowly pour in the milk, whisking constantly, until thickened, about 5 minutes. Remove from the heat and add 1 cup (100 g) of the Parmesan and the Gruyère cheese, whisking until the cheese is melted. Add the kale mixture and stir until well combined.

Preheat the oven to 375°F (190°C). Allow the dough to rest on the counter for 5 minutes to soften up a bit. Meanwhile, on a large, lightly floured piece of parchment paper, roll the dough into a 15-inch (38 cm) round. Transfer to a rimmed baking sheet. Pile the kale filling in the center of the dough, leaving a 2-inch (5 cm) border around all sides. Fold the border over the edge of the filling, pleating as you go and pressing down gently to seal. In a small bowl, mix the egg with 1 teaspoon water; brush the dough with the egg wash and sprinkle with the remaining ¼ cup (25 g) Parmesan cheese.
Bake until the filling is bubbling and the crust is golden brown, about 45 minutes. Allow to cool slightly, then zest a fresh lemon over the top. Cut into wedges and serve.

*Makes one 10-inch (25 cm) crostata/Serves 6+*

# *Dad's Sun-Dried Tomato, Parmesan & Roasted* Garlic-Herb Bread

*Recently my dad has taken up bread baking. It's pretty much the best hobby because I almost always get fresh bread whenever I see him. (Even better is when he makes me a grilled cheese with that said bread—hello, pages 116 and 119.) Anyway, he's become somewhat of a professional, but luckily he still takes my suggestions. So one day we stuffed one of the loaves with some of my favorite flavors and the result was nothing short of mind-blowing.*

---

### Ingredients

6 cups plus 6 tablespoons (800 g) all-purpose white flour

1⅔ cups (200 g) whole-wheat flour

3 cups (725 g) warm water (90 to 95°F/32 to 35°C)

2 tablespoons plus 2 teaspoons (22 grams) kosher salt

1¼ teaspoons instant dried yeast

1 cup (110 g) sun-dried tomatoes, drained of any oil, roughly chopped

¾ cup (about 195 g) Whole Roasted Garlic (page 251), drained of any oil, roughly chopped

2 cups (200 g) grated Parmesan cheese

¼ cup (11 g) fresh thyme leaves

Combine both flours and the warm water in a large bowl. Cover and let rest for 20 minutes. Sprinkle the salt and yeast over the top of the flour mixture along with the sun-dried tomatoes, garlic, Parmesan, and thyme. Mix the dough to evenly incorporate; let sit for 15 minutes.

Fold the dough into quadrants, reshape into a ball, and rest for 30 minutes. Fold again and then cover and let rest for an additional 4 hours 15 minutes at room temperature, until it roughly triples in size. If you leave the dough near sunlight, it will rise slightly faster.

After resting, turn the dough onto a lightly floured surface and cut it in half. Shape the dough into 2 tight balls and place them seam side down in a proofing basket. If you don't have a floured proofing basket, place the dough in a clean metal bowl that you have dusted with flour. Cover and let proof for 1 hour 15 minutes.

While the dough is proofing, preheat the oven to 450°F (230°C). Place 2 large heavy-bottom Dutch ovens in the oven to heat on the middle rack for 30 minutes.

Carefully remove the dough from the baskets, remove the pots from the oven, and place each ball of dough into a Dutch oven, seam side up, and cover with the top. Bake for 25 minutes, then remove the lids, and bake for an additional 15 to 20 minutes. The bread should be golden brown on top when done.

*Makes 2 loaves*

# Jerk Chicken Burger

*The first vacation Thomas and I ever went on was to Jamaica back in our college days. We fell in love with smoky, super-spiced jerk chicken. Learning how to make it at home—which is as easy as mixing together a bunch of spices—was definitely the best souvenir from the trip. I think the seasoning really shines with chicken, but this would work with turkey or beef too. Top the burger with some mango slaw and call it a day. You could also swap the bun for a lettuce wrap, if that's more your speed.*

---

Ingredients

For the burgers

5 cloves garlic, minced

2 teaspoons brown sugar

1½ tablespoons fresh grated ginger

2 tablespoons soy sauce or Worcestershire sauce

2 tablespoons fresh lime juice

2 sprigs thyme leaves, minced (about 2 teaspoons)

1 teaspoon ground allspice

½ teaspoon ground cinnamon

¼ teaspoon ground nutmeg

2 teaspoons kosher salt

2 teaspoons orange zest

1 teaspoon cayenne pepper

1½ pounds (680 g) ground chicken thigh

⅔ cup (55 g) panko bread crumbs

For the mango slaw

1 cup (165 g) cubed ripe mango, then small-diced

2 cups (190 g) shredded red cabbage

½ cup (20 g) chopped fresh cilantro

3 tablespoons olive oil

¼ cup (60 ml) fresh lime juice

Kosher salt and freshly cracked black pepper

For the scallion crème

1 cup (240 ml) Greek yogurt or labneh

1 clove garlic, minced

½ cup (50 g) chopped scallions

Kosher salt and freshly cracked black pepper

2 tablespoons neutral oil, plus more as needed, for cooking

4 brioche buns, for serving

To make the burgers: In a large bowl, combine all the burger ingredients and mix until thoroughly combined. Refrigerate for 1 hour.

Meanwhile, make the mango slaw: In a medium bowl, combine the mango, cabbage, cilantro, olive oil, and lime juice and toss to coat. Season to taste with salt and pepper. Set aside until ready to use.

To make the scallion crème: In a small bowl, stir together the yogurt, garlic, and scallions. Season to taste with salt and pepper.

Shape the chicken mixture into 4 patties and season with more salt. Warm the oil in a large skillet or grill pan over high heat. Sear the burgers until well browned and the internal temperature reaches 165°F (75°C), about 7 minutes per side. Transfer to a plate while you toast the buns. Add more oil to the pan if necessary. Place the buns cut side down in the skillet and toast for 3 minutes, or until golden brown. To assemble the burgers, spread scallion crème on the bottom buns. Top with the chicken burger, slaw, and the tops of the buns.

*Serves 4*

# Throw an Outdoor Bash

This is the ultimate menu for your summer entertaining needs, whether you're hosting a pool party or an old-school neighborhood potluck. I took classic cookout favorites and elevated them just a touch, plus added in some DIY moments so your guests can get in on the fun.

———————

Smashed Cheeseburger Bar

Hot Dog Bar

Watermelon Salad

Chips & My Favorite Ceviche

Strawberry Cheesecake Ice Cream Sandwiches

Sparkling Blackberry Lemonade Pops

California Dreaming Coconut Cocktail

Aperol Spritz

*Serves 6 to 8*

# Smashed Cheeseburger Bar

**Ingredients**
2 pounds (910 g) ground beef (80% lean)
1 tablespoon garlic powder
½ tablespoon onion powder
Kosher salt and freshly cracked black pepper
8 slices of your favorite cheese
Grilled brioche hamburger buns

In a large bowl, combine the ground beef with the garlic powder, onion powder, salt, and pepper and mix to combine. Divide the mixture into 8 portions and form very thin patties. Heat an outdoor grill to medium-high heat. Arrange all the patties on the grill and cook for about 4 minutes on the first side until charred. Flip and cook for an additional 2 to 3 minutes. Add a slice of cheese on top of each patty and let the cheese melt for about 1 minute. Transfer the burgers to a part of the grill with indirect heat to keep warm.

Assemble the burger bar toppings and let everyone DIY their own adventure.

# Hot Dog Bar

- Grilled hot dogs
- Grilled brioche buns

**Burger and hot dog bar toppings**

- Sautéed onions and peppers with shredded Fontina cheese

- Crispy bacon, warmed pinto beans, diced onions, shredded Cheddar, pico de gallo, pickled jalapeños

- Ketchup and mustard and diced onions

- Diced pineapple, chopped grilled red onions, sautéed padron peppers, teriyaki sauce

- BBQ sauce and coleslaw

- Gaby's Famous Guacamole (page 257), charred corn, and Pico de Gallo (page 257)

In a small bowl, whisk together the remaining 2 tablespoons of olive oil, the vinegar, garlic, and remaining finely chopped shallots and season to taste with salt and pepper.

When ready to serve, add the cubed feta, cucumber, and thinly sliced shallot to the salad. Toss to combine. Transfer to a serving platter, drizzle with the vinaigrette, and top with more torn mint, whole mint leaves, and basil.

# Chips & My Favorite Ceviche

## Ingredients
1 shallot, finely diced

⅓ cup (75 ml) fresh lime juice, plus more as needed

¼ cup (60 ml) fresh orange juice

1 teaspoon crushed red pepper flakes

8 ounces (225 g) best-quality skinless, boneless sea bass fillet, cut into ½-inch (12 mm) pieces

8 ounces (225 g) rock shrimp, halved lengthwise, or small shrimp, peeled, deveined, cut into ½-inch (12 mm) pieces

Kosher salt

2 tablespoons olive oil

¾ cup (125 g) diced mango

½ cup (150 g) diced cucumber

1 ripe avocado, pitted, peeled, and diced

¼ cup (30 g) diced red onion

½ jalapeño chile, finely chopped

2 tablespoons chopped fresh chives

Freshly cracked black pepper

In a large bowl, combine the shallot, lime juice, orange juice, and red pepper flakes and stir. Add the sea bass and shrimp, season with salt, and gently stir to combine so all the fish is coated in the citrus juice. Cover and refrigerate for at least 1 hour or up to 3 hours, until the fish cooks in the acid.

The seafood is ready when it looks fully "cooked." This means that each piece of fish no longer looks raw when split open. If the fish still looks slightly raw, cover and place back in the refrigerator for an additional hour.

To serve, drain the fish of the remaining juice and add the olive oil, along with the mango, cucumber, avocado, red onion, jalapeño, and chives and gently toss to combine. Taste and season with additional salt, pepper, or lime juice as needed. Serve immediately.

# Watermelon Salad

## Ingredients
1 small seedless watermelon, cut into 1-inch (2.5 cm) cubes

2 shallots, finely chopped

¼ cup (13 g) torn fresh mint, plus extra for garnish

¼ cup (60 ml) plus 2 tablespoons olive oil

Kosher salt and freshly cracked black pepper

3 tablespoons red wine vinegar

3 cloves garlic, chopped

1 (5-ounce/140 g package) feta cheese, drained, cut into ½-inch (12 mm) cubes

1 large English cucumber, cut into large dice

1 shallot, thinly sliced

Fresh mint, whole leaves

Fresh basil, whole leaves

Combine the watermelon, half of the finely chopped shallots, and ¼ cup (13 g) of the torn mint in a large bowl and add ¼ cup (60 ml) of the olive oil. Season with salt and pepper and toss to combine. Transfer to the fridge and let marinate for at least 1 hour or up to 3 hours.

# Strawberry Cheesecake Ice Cream Sandwiches

## Ingredients

1 cup (225 g/2 sticks) unsalted butter, at room temperature

1½ cups (300 g) granulated sugar

½ cup (110 g) packed brown sugar

2 large eggs

2½ teaspoons pure vanilla extract

2½ cups (215 g) all-purpose flour

1 teaspoon kosher salt

1 teaspoon baking soda

1 teaspoon baking powder

1½ cups (25 g) freeze-dried strawberries, roughly chopped

½ cup (85 g) white chocolate chips

No-Churn Mascarpone Strawberry Ice Cream (page 245)

Cream together the butter and both sugars in a stand mixer. Mix in the eggs and vanilla, making sure to scrape down the sides of the bowl with a spatula. Add the flour, salt, baking soda, and baking powder and mix on low speed until everything is incorporated. Fold in most of the freeze-dried strawberries and white chocolate chips, reserving a little bit of each to top the cookies with before baking.

Chill the dough in the refrigerator for 2 hours. When ready to bake, preheat the oven to 350°F (175°C). Line a baking sheet with parchment paper.

Scoop out 2 tablespoons of dough and roll it into a ball. Place just 8 to 10 balls on the prepared baking sheet, as they will spread due to their large size. Top each unbaked cookie with a few extra white chocolate chips and freeze-dried strawberries and push them into the dough to stick.

Bake for 11 to 12 minutes, until the cookies are just slightly golden around the edges. Let rest on the baking sheet. If you want to flatten them out to make them bigger, carefully bang the baking sheet on the counter to release any excess air in the cookies. After a 10-minute rest on the baking sheet, remove them to a cooling rack and cool completely before transferring to the freezer to harden up.

Once chilled, place a few scoops of the no-churn mascarpone strawberry ice cream onto one of the cookies and sandwich another cookie on top. Serve immediately or store in the freezer until you're ready to serve.

# Sparkling Blackberry Lemonade Pops

## Ingredients

3 cups (720 ml) lemonade

10 blackberries

½ cup (120 ml) prosecco

In a blender, puree the lemonade and blackberries until smooth. Add the prosecco and stir to combine.

Divide the mixture among paper cups or an ice pop mold. Place a colorful straw or wooden pop stick into each cup.

Place a small piece of tinfoil over each cup, cutting out a small hole for the straw. This will ensure that the straw stays straight while freezing. Transfer to a freezer and freeze the pops until firm, about 8 hours.

# California Dreaming Coconut Cocktail

**Ingredients**

6 ounces (180 ml) cream of coconut

24 ounces (720 ml) pineapple juice

12 ounces (360 ml) dark rum

6 ounces (180 ml) fresh orange juice

Fresh pineapple wedges

Combine the coconut cream, pineapple juice, rum, and orange juice in a blender and blend until smooth. Serve over ice with pineapple as garnish.

# Aperol Spritz

**Ingredients**

16 ounces (480 ml) Aperol

24 ounces (720 ml) dry prosecco

Club soda or unflavored sparkling water

Orange slices

Into 6 to 8 glasses, add ice until nearly full. Pour in equal amounts of the Aperol followed by equal amounts of the prosecco. Top off with a splash of club soda and an orange slice. Stir and enjoy!

# Chapter 5
# When In Doubt . . . Vacation

I could tell you that I love to travel because it means meeting new people, experiencing new cultures, and seeing new parts of the world—and that's all true—but we all know that the real reason to hit the road is to eat. A lot. I love trying different foods and flavor combinations and then bringing them home to play with in my kitchen. This also means that I can scratch the vacation itch by cooking with these ingredients any time I want. So until I can get to the far-flung places I've been dying to go to (Thailand, Japan, and India) or revisit old favorites (Italy, France, and Greece), I can reach for any one of the recipes in this chapter and travel the world from the comfort of my own home.

# *Cauliflower* Shawarma Bowl

*I originally came up with this recipe as a side dish (page 194), serving the cauliflower on its own, because it really is that good. It has all the rich, crispy flavor of a meat-based shawarma, which is perfect for a Middle Eastern street food–style bowl with fresh veggies, hummus, feta, and tahini dressing. Serve it with pita chips and you have yourself a meal.*

---

### Ingredients

2 pounds (910 g) cauliflower florets

1 tablespoon ground turmeric

1 tablespoon ground cumin

1 teaspoon kosher salt

1 teaspoon freshly cracked black pepper

1 teaspoon ground coriander

1 teaspoon paprika

¼ cup (60 ml) olive oil

1 cup (240 g) hummus (page 51)

1 cup (55 g) shredded romaine lettuce

1 cup (95 g) shredded purple cabbage

1 cup (145 g) cherry tomatoes, halved

1 cup (120 g) sliced Persian cucumbers (about 1 cucumber)

½ cup (75 g) crumbled feta cheese

1 cup (240 ml) Lemon Tahini Dressing (page 252)

Toasted pita chips

Preheat the oven to 425°F (220°C). Line a baking sheet with parchment paper.

Put the cauliflower florets on the prepared baking sheet. In a medium bowl, combine the turmeric, cumin, salt, pepper, coriander, paprika, and olive oil and stir to blend. Drizzle the spiced oil on top of the cauliflower and toss to combine so the florets are evenly coated. Roast for 35 minutes, or until the cauliflower is caramelized and browned.

To assemble the bowls, schmear ¼ cup (60 g) of the hummus in the bottom of 4 bowls. Top the hummus with equal amounts of the romaine, cabbage, tomatoes, and cucumbers. Pile about ¾ cup (245 g) of the roasted cauliflower in the middle of each bowl and sprinkle with the feta. Drizzle with 4 tablespoons of the lemon tahini dressing and serve toasted pita wedges alongside to scoop up anything you want!

*Serves 4*

# Pad Thai

*The key to recreating authentic-ish Asian food at home is layering flavors—most of which you already have in your pantry. The two standout ingredients here are fish sauce and tamarind paste, which together bring this dish to life. The fish sauce is a little salty and a little funky, but you won't taste fish, only deep, salty savoriness. Then the sweet-sour tamarind paste brightens everything up. And while it may look like there's a lot to this dish with all its ingredients, I promise that it takes no time to throw together, making it one of my favorite takeout-replacing weeknight meals.*

## Ingredients

1 pound (455 g) pad thai or rice noodles

5 tablespoons sesame oil

2 cloves garlic, roughly chopped

4 scallions, sliced into 1-inch (2.5 cm) pieces

3 tablespoons soy sauce

3 tablespoons rice vinegar

3 tablespoons fish sauce (optional)

3 tablespoons tamarind paste

¼ cup (50 g) sugar

1 teaspoon red pepper flakes

Juice of 1 lime

2 large eggs

1 cup (110 g) julienned carrots

1 cup (100 g) mung bean sprouts

½ cup (70 g) chopped peanuts

½ cup (20 g) chopped fresh cilantro

Lime wedges

Sriracha

Cook the noodles according to package instructions. Toss lightly with 2 tablespoons of the sesame oil to prevent sticking; set aside.

In a large skillet over medium-high heat, warm the remaining 3 tablespoons sesame oil. Add the garlic and scallions and cook for 2 minutes. Add the soy sauce, rice vinegar, fish sauce, if using, tamarind paste, sugar, red pepper flakes, and lime juice and whisk until smooth. Continue to cook until the sauce is slightly thickened, about 5 minutes.

Add the cooked noodles and toss well to coat. Push the noodles to one side of the skillet, then crack the eggs into the pan and stir with a wooden spoon, breaking up the eggs until fully cooked, about 3 minutes. Fold the eggs into the noodles. Add ½ cup (55 g) of the carrots, ½ cup (50 g) of the bean sprouts, and ¼ cup (35 g) of the peanuts, stir to coat, and continue to cook for 3 minutes, or until the vegetables are warmed through.

Top with the remaining carrots, sprouts, peanuts, and the chopped cilantro. Serve with lime wedges and a drizzle of sriracha.

*Serves 6*

# *Salmon Larb* Coconut Rice Bowls

*In my last cookbook, I included a chicken larb that was easily in the top five most-made, most-talked-about recipes from the book. That larb should have had its own Instagram account for all the traffic it got. Shortly after the book came out, I was cooking with one of my favorite humans on the planet, Geri, and we decided to get a little crazy with larb. We ended up swapping out the chicken for seafood, and we both agreed that this might—somehow—be even better than the original.*

---

## Ingredients

### For the quick pickles

3 Persian cucumbers, thinly sliced
1 cup (95 g) shredded purple cabbage
1 cup (70 g) shredded napa cabbage
½ red onion, thinly sliced
3 tablespoons rice wine vinegar

### For the salmon

2 tablespoons rice wine vinegar
2 tablespoons sambal oelek
½ teaspoon soy sauce
¼ teaspoon sesame oil
3 cloves garlic, roughly chopped
1 (1-inch/2.5 cm) piece fresh ginger, peeled and finely chopped
1½ pounds (680 g) salmon, skinned, pin bones removed

### For serving

Coconut Rice (recipe follows)
Fresh mint, basil, and cilantro leaves
Sliced scallions

**To make the quick pickles:** In a small bowl, toss the cucumbers, purple and napa cabbages, red onion, and vinegar. Set aside to marinate while you cook the salmon. Toss every few minutes to ensure the vinegar is evenly coating the vegetables.

**To make the salmon:** In a small bowl, combine the rice wine vinegar, sambal oelek, soy sauce, sesame oil, garlic, and ginger. Stir to blend. Place the salmon on a foil-lined baking sheet and carefully slather the marinade on top of the salmon. Let sit for at least 30 minutes or up to 4 hours in the refrigerator.

When ready to cook, turn the oven to broil and broil the salmon for 8 to 10 minutes, until cooked through and golden on top. Remove from the oven and let rest. Flake before serving.

To assemble, divide the rice among 4 bowls, followed by the flaked salmon and quick pickled cabbage and cucumber mixture. Top with plenty of fresh mint, basil, cilantro, and scallions. Serve immediately.

*Serves 4*

## Coconut Rice

1 cup (240 ml) coconut milk
1 teaspoon sugar
1 teaspoon kosher salt
2 cups (360 g) jasmine rice
Zest and juice of 1 lime

In a medium saucepan over medium-high heat, combine 2 cups (480 ml) water, the coconut milk, sugar, and salt and bring to a simmer. Add the rice and bring back to a low simmer. Cover the pot, reduce the heat to low, and cook undisturbed for about 15 minutes, until all the liquid has been absorbed. Turn off the heat and let the rice steam for another 5 to 10 minutes, until fully cooked and soft. Uncover, fluff the rice, and toss in the lime zest and juice.

# *Ground Pork* Red Curry Bowl

*I'm all about that curry life, especially on nights when it's a little chilly and I just want to curl up with a bowl of comfort food and a TV show (or three). I love making this recipe because it comes together in no time, the base is creamy and rich thanks to coconut milk, and all it needs is a squeeze of lime to make all the flavors really pop.*

## Ingredients

1 tablespoon coconut oil

1 red onion, finely diced

1 jalapeño chile, finely diced

6 scallions, sliced

4 cloves garlic, finely minced

1 (1-inch/2.5 cm) piece fresh ginger, peeled and finely minced

1 pound (455 g) ground pork (ground chicken or turkey work too)

2 tablespoons red curry paste

Kosher salt

1 (15-ounce/430 g) can full-fat coconut milk

Coconut Rice (page 150)

2 cups (195 g) shredded cabbage

Fresh cilantro sprigs

Lime wedges

Heat the coconut oil in a large Dutch oven or skillet over medium-high heat. Once melted, add the red onion and jalapeño and sauté for 5 to 7 minutes, until the onion is translucent. Add half of the scallions, the garlic, and ginger and sauté for 2 minutes, or until fragrant. Add the ground pork and cook, breaking it up with the back of a wooden spoon. Add the red curry paste and continue to cook until no pink remains; season with salt. Pour in the coconut milk and stir to combine. Bring to a boil, reduce to a simmer, and let simmer for 10 minutes, or until thickened. Remove from the heat, add the remaining scallions, and stir to combine.

To serve, divide the rice into 4 bowls with equal amounts of the pork and shredded cabbage. Top with plenty of fresh cilantro and freshly squeezed lime juice. Season with salt as needed. Serve immediately.

*Serves 4*

# *Healthy* Bibimbap Bowls

*There's nothing unhealthy about bibimbap, but what's so great about my take on it—it's a brilliant excuse to clean out all the random veggies that you have lying around in your fridge. This is also the perfect dish to make when you need something super hearty and filling. It could feed two very hungry people or four civilized normal people . . . but let's just say I'm not one of those.*

---

### Ingredients

1 tablespoon gochujang (red chile paste)

1 tablespoon toasted sesame oil

2 teaspoons soy sauce

2 cups (400 g) short-grain white rice, rinsed

2 tablespoons seasoned rice vinegar

Kosher salt

2 carrots, thinly shaved

½ cup (120 ml) plain sesame oil

1 pound (455 g) assorted wild mushrooms, stemmed and sliced

1 (5-ounce/140 g) bag baby spinach

1 tablespoon vegetable oil

2 to 4 eggs

2 tablespoons kimchi

1 cup (100 g) mung bean sprouts

3 radishes, thinly sliced

1 tablespoon black and/or white sesame seeds

In a small bowl, stir together the gochujang, toasted sesame oil, 1 tablespoon water, and the soy sauce. Set aside.

In a medium saucepan, combine the rice and 2½ cups (600 ml) water. Bring to a boil, then reduce the heat to a simmer, cover, and cook for 15 minutes. Remove from the heat, fluff with a fork, and season with 1 tablespoon of the seasoned rice wine vinegar and salt to taste; set aside. In a small bowl, combine the shaved carrots and remaining 1 tablespoon of seasoned rice vinegar; set aside.

In a large skillet over medium-high heat, warm ¼ cup (60 ml) of the plain sesame oil. Add the mushrooms in a single layer and cook, stirring occasionally, until well browned and caramelized, about 10 minutes. In another skillet over medium heat, warm 1 tablespoon of the plain sesame oil. Add the spinach and cook until wilted, about 5 minutes. Keep warm.

When ready to serve, warm the remaining 3 tablespoons sesame oil in a large skillet over high heat. Add the cooked rice and use the back of a spatula to press the rice firmly into the pan. Allow to cook for 5 minutes, then flip the rice over, breaking up some of the pieces into smaller ones, but being sure to leave some large crispy pieces. Cook an additional 5 minutes.

Meanwhile, in a medium skillet, warm the vegetable oil. Add the eggs and fry until the whites are set but the yolks are still runny, about 4 minutes.

To assemble the bibimbap, divide the rice among bowls. Top with the sautéed mushrooms, spinach, carrots, kimchi, bean sprouts, and radishes. Drizzle with the gochujang sauce and top with the fried eggs and sesame seeds.

*Serves 2 to 4*

# Matt's Shortcut Mole Nachos

*Mole is a PAIN IN THE ASS TO MAKE. Usually. But not this one—it doesn't require you to go to 14,567 stores to track down a bunch of hard-to-find ingredients; it doesn't take 1,000 years to make, AND it's so velvety and creamy that you could slather it on nachos and not even need any melted cheese. But then again, you never really need cheese . . .*

## Ingredients

### For the mole

1 cup (110 g) chopped yellow onion

3 cloves garlic, chopped

2 whole chipotle peppers from a can of chipotles in adobo

2 tablespoons extra-virgin olive oil

1 teaspoon ground cumin

1 teaspoon ground coriander

1 teaspoon dried Mexican oregano

½ teaspoon ground cinnamon

½ teaspoon ground allspice

1 cup (240 ml) tomato puree

2 tablespoons semisweet chocolate chips

1 tablespoon creamy peanut butter

Kosher salt and freshly cracked pepper

¼ to ½ cup (60 to 120 ml) warm water

### For the nachos

1 (12-ounce/340 g) bag of tortilla chips

3 cups (585 g) shredded rotisserie chicken, warmed

½ cup (120 ml) crema Mexicana or sour cream

½ cup (50 g) queso fresco

6 scallions, sliced

¼ cup (10 g) roughly chopped fresh cilantro

4 radishes, sliced paper thin

**To make the mole:** Combine the onion, garlic, chipotles, and 2 tablespoons water in a high-powered blender or food processor. Process until completely smooth.

Heat the olive oil in a medium nonstick skillet over medium-high heat. Once the oil is shimmering, add the pureed onion mixture; it will pop and sizzle. Stir over medium-high heat for 3 minutes, or until it thickens up. Add the cumin, coriander, oregano, cinnamon, and allspice and continue to cook for another minute.

Reduce the heat to low, add the tomato puree, chocolate chips, and peanut butter, and cook for 3 minutes. Season with salt and pepper. Remove from the heat and thin the mole to your desired consistency with the warm water.

**To build the nachos:** Preheat the oven to 350°F (175°C) and line a baking sheet with aluminum foil or parchment paper. Lay half of the tortilla chips on the pan, drizzle half of the mole over the chips, and top with half of the chicken. Repeat with the remaining chips, mole, and chicken.

Bake the nachos for 5 to 8 minutes. You want everything nice and warm. Remove from the oven and dollop with the crema Mexicana and queso fresco and sprinkle the scallions, cilantro, and sliced radishes on top.

*Serves 4 to 6*

# Butter Chicken
## with Roti

*There are few people in the world who I will blindly trust to pick a restaurant when we're going out to eat, and Adam is one of those people. He knows what's up, and last year he took me to this incredible fast-casual restaurant that served roti. It was my first time eating this buttery, chewy Indian flatbread, and let me tell you, it most certainly was not the last. I developed my own recipe so I can make it any time I need to sop up all the saucy goodness of this butter chicken, one of the best Indian dishes that exists (IMHO).*

### Ingredients

2 pounds (910 g) skinless boneless chicken thighs, cut into 1-inch (2.5 cm) pieces

1 cup (240 ml) Greek yogurt

2 tablespoons fresh lemon juice, plus more as needed

1½ tablespoons ground turmeric

2 tablespoons garam masala

2 tablespoons ground cumin

1 teaspoon cayenne pepper

½ cup (115 g/1 stick) unsalted butter

1 onion, cut into small dice

4 cloves garlic, roughly chopped

2 tablespoons grated fresh ginger

1 (15-ounce/430 g) can diced tomatoes

½ cup (120 ml) chicken broth

3 cups (720 ml) heavy cream

1 teaspoon tomato paste

Kosher salt

Fresh cilantro leaves

Roti (recipe follows) or store-bought pita bread

Put the chicken, Greek yogurt, and lemon juice in a bowl, add the turmeric, garam masala, cumin, and cayenne and marinate overnight in the refrigerator.

Melt the butter in a large skillet over medium heat. Stir in the onion and cook slowly until it is translucent. Add the garlic and ginger and cook until fragrant, 2 to 3 minutes more. Add the tomatoes to the skillet and cook for 5 minutes. Add the chicken and its marinade to the pan and cook for 5 minutes. Season with salt. Add the chicken broth and bring the mixture to a boil, then lower the heat and simmer for 30 minutes. Stir in the heavy cream and tomato paste and continue to simmer until the chicken has cooked through and the sauce is thick, about 15 minutes.

Taste, adjust the seasoning as needed, adding more lemon juice for a bit of acid. Garnish with cilantro leaves and serve alongside the roti bread (or store-bought pita).

*Serves 4 to 6*

Continued

# Roti

**3¾ cups (425 g) cake flour, plus extra for rolling**
**½ teaspoon salt**
**2 tablespoons vegetable oil**
**2 tablespoons butter or ghee**

In a stand mixer fitted with the paddle attachment, combine the flour, salt, and vegetable oil. In a small saucepan over high heat, bring 1 cup (240 ml) plus 2 tablespoons water just to a boil. With the mixer on low speed, carefully pour in the boiling water and mix for 1 minute. Switch to the dough hook and knead on low for 5 minutes, or until the dough is silky smooth and soft. Remove the mixer bowl from the stand, cover with a clean towel, and let the dough rest for 5 to 10 minutes. The dough can be made a day in advance; just wrap in plastic wrap and keep in the refrigerator. Let sit at room temperature for 15 minutes before rolling and cooking.

Melt the butter in a small bowl and have a pastry brush ready.

Turn the dough out onto a lightly floured surface and give it a quick knead by hand. Tear off a chunk of dough slightly larger than a golf ball, about 2½ inches (6 cm), and cover the remaining dough with plastic wrap. Shape your piece of dough into a flat disk, and working with a well-floured rolling pin, begin to roll the dough into a large circle, about 10 inches (25 cm) in diameter. Use as much flour as needed to prevent sticking.

Brush the dough circle with a thin layer of melted butter. Working from the farthest edge from you, start rolling the dough toward you. You'll want a "snake" about 10 inches (25 cm) in length. Cut the roll into 4 equal pieces.

Take one piece and cover the remaining pieces with plastic wrap. Stand the piece of dough cut side up and smash it down into a disk. With floured hands, work the dough into a small disk about 2 inches (5 cm) wide. Start rolling the disk into a circle about 5 to 6 inches (12 to 15 cm) in diameter, as thin as you can make it, adding flour as needed to prevent sticking.

Move the roti to a baking sheet lined with plastic wrap and cover with another piece of plastic wrap to prevent it from drying out while you roll the remaining roti.

Heat a large nonstick pan over high heat; you'll want it VERY hot. Place one roti in the pan, wait a few seconds, until you see small bubbles forming, then flip. Continue to rotate and flip the roti until dark brown spots show up, for a total cooking time of less than 1 minute. Puffing up is a good sign; you can smash the roti down with a spatula. Remove from the pan and keep warm in a towel while you repeat the process. You can also give the hot roti a quick brush with butter if you like.

# Dal Veggie Bowls

*Indian food is one of my favorite things to order when we get takeout, and it's almost always dal, aka lentils stewed with spices until they're rich and creamy. Turns out, it's simple enough to make at home, and you can double the recipe and feed a small army.*

---

### Ingredients

2 tablespoons coconut oil

1 jalapeño chile, finely diced

2 tablespoons finely chopped fresh ginger

1 yellow onion, thinly sliced

4 cloves garlic, finely chopped

1 teaspoon ground turmeric

1 teaspoon curry powder

3 tablespoons red curry paste

1½ cups (360 ml) coconut milk

1 (14.5-ounce/415 g) can fire-roasted diced tomatoes

1 cup (200 g) red lentils

Kosher salt and freshly cracked black pepper

2 cups (400 g) cooked quinoa, couscous, or other grain

Chopped fresh cilantro

Lemon or lime wedges

Heat the coconut oil in a medium heavy-bottom pot or Dutch oven over medium-high heat. Once hot, add the jalapeño, ginger, onion, and garlic. Sauté for 5 minutes, or until the onion starts to get translucent and fragrant. Add the turmeric, curry powder, and curry paste and sauté for another 1 minute to toast. Add the coconut milk, ½ cup (120 ml) water, and the entire can of diced tomatoes. Stir to combine. Add the lentils, cover the pot, reduce the heat to medium, and let the lentils cook for 20 to 25 minutes, until soft. Remove from the heat and season with salt and pepper to taste.

Serve over quinoa, couscous, or any other grain of your choosing, with plenty of cilantro on top and lemon or lime juice, depending on your preference. Also great to throw in some leftover roasted veggies like roasted broccolini and roasted sweet potatoes.

*Serves 4*

# *Pork Meatball*
# Bahn Mi Rice Bowl

*For my version, I took the super-succulent and flavorful pork and turned it into a meatball, added in a quick-pickled carrot, then heaped it all on top of rice (instead of a roll) with traditional toppings like chiles, fresh cilantro, and cucumber.*

---

### Ingredients

**For the quick-pickled carrots**

3 carrots, peeled and sliced into thin batons

½ cup (120 ml) rice vinegar

1 teaspoon black peppercorns

1 teaspoon mustard seeds (optional)

3 tablespoons sugar

2 teaspoons kosher salt

**For the meatballs**

1½ pounds (680 g) ground pork

4 cloves garlic, minced

1 tablespoon minced fresh ginger

3 scallions, thinly sliced

2 teaspoons fish sauce

2 teaspoons soy sauce

¼ cup (30 g) panko bread crumbs

Pinch of sugar

Kosher salt and freshly cracked black pepper

¼ cup (60 ml) sesame oil

**For the rice and toppings**

2 cups (390 ml) white rice, rinsed

1 cucumber, sliced on the bias

1 bunch fresh cilantro

1 jalapeño chile, sliced

1 Fresno chile, sliced

4 radishes, thinly shaved

Soy sauce

**To make the quick-pickled carrots:** Place the carrots in a shallow bowl. In a liquid measuring cup, whisk together the vinegar, peppercorns, mustard seeds, if using, sugar, and salt. Pour the brine over the carrots, making sure the carrots are fully submerged in the liquid. Cover and refrigerate for at least 1 hour. Drain, discarding the brine.

**To make the meatballs:** In a large bowl, combine the pork, garlic, ginger, scallions, fish sauce, soy sauce, bread crumbs, sugar, salt, and pepper. Mix until thoroughly combined and refrigerate for 30 minutes. Once chilled, shape into 1½-inch (4 cm) meatballs.

Preheat the oven to 400°F (205°C). In a large skillet over high heat, warm the sesame oil. In batches, sear the meatballs until well browned on all sides, about 6 minutes per batch. Transfer to the oven and heat until the internal temperature of the meatballs reaches 145°F (63°C), about 5 minutes. Cover with aluminum foil to keep warm.

**To make the rice and finish the dish:** While the meatballs are cooking, in a medium pot, combine the rice with 3 cups (720 ml) water. Bring to a boil over high heat. Cover, reduce the heat to low, and cook for 15 minutes. Fluff with a fork. Cover to keep warm.

Divide the rice evenly among 4 bowls. Top with the meatballs, cucumber slices, cilantro, chile peppers, radishes, pickled carrots, and a drizzle of soy sauce.

*Serves 4*

# Helen's
# Beef Picadillo

*Picadillo is a Spanish/Latin hash that uses ground beef with any number of veggies mixed in, but everyone has their own special version. I'm particularly partial to Matt's mom's, which brings a Tex-Mex vibe through potatoes, jalapeños, and all sorts of spices. I highly recommend serving this up with plenty of fresh tortillas—just like Helen, Matt's mom. And if you want to serve it with a sprinkle of cheese, do it, just don't tell Matt I told you!*

## Ingredients

5 Roma tomatoes, roughly chopped
1 cup (240 ml) chicken broth
1 tablespoon olive oil
1 pound (455 g) ground beef
1 pound (455 g) ground pork
1 yellow onion, roughly chopped
4 cloves garlic, roughly chopped
2 medium carrots, roughly chopped
1 medium-large russet potato, peeled and chopped
2 jalapeño chiles, finely chopped
1 tablespoon chili powder
1 teaspoon ground cumin
1 teaspoon dried oregano
Kosher salt and freshly cracked black pepper
¼ cup (35 g) frozen peas
¼ cup (10 g) chopped fresh cilantro
Flour tortillas
Shredded Cheddar cheese (optional)

Put the tomatoes and chicken broth in a blender and puree until smooth. Set aside.

In a large heavy-bottom pan, heat the olive oil over medium-high heat. Add the ground beef and ground pork and cook, breaking it into pieces with a wooden spoon, until browned. Add the onion, garlic, carrots, potatoes, and jalapeños and sauté for 8 to 10 minutes, until the carrots and potatoes start to cook down. Stir in the chili powder, cumin, and oregano and season with salt and pepper. Mix in the reserved tomato mixture and bring to a boil. Cover the pan, reduce the heat to a simmer, and cook for 10 to 15 minutes, until the carrots and potatoes are fully cooked.

Stir in the frozen peas, adjust the salt to taste, and add in the cilantro. Serve warm with your favorite tortillas and shredded Cheddar, if using, for topping.

*Serves 4*

# Chapter 6

# So Easy Even Thomas Can Do It

When I met my husband back in our college days, the man was eating nothing but frozen pizza and hot pockets. It was a sad sight, and I knew that I had my work cut out for me. I've since introduced him to tons of different kinds of foods and flavors, which he thankfully loves. I'm also fairly certain he's developed a more refined palate than me—it's pretty professional—but that still doesn't mean that he's a seasoned cook. Luckily, I've taught him a thing or two, which is why he can get by when I'm not home to make dinner. This chapter is dedicated to the recipes of mine that he feels comfortable cooking as a novice in the kitchen, plus a few Thomas originals. If he can do it, anyone can.

# Broccoli Beef

*Finding GREAT broccoli beef to order in can be hard. So I vowed to come up with my own take on it that never disappoints. The ingredients are easy to come by, you can use good-quality meat, and you'll have leftovers for days.*

---

## Ingredients

1 pound (455 g) flank steak, cut into 1-inch (2.5 cm) strips

½ teaspoon kosher salt

½ teaspoon ground white pepper

½ cup (120 ml) soy sauce

3 tablespoons brown sugar

5 cloves garlic, minced

1 (1-inch/2.5 cm) piece fresh ginger, peeled and grated

1 tablespoon cornstarch (optional)

3 tablespoons sesame oil

½ yellow onion, sliced

1 large head broccoli, cut into florets and blanched

Cooked rice

1 tablespoon toasted sesame seeds

3 scallions, sliced on the bias

Season the beef with the salt and white pepper. In a small bowl, whisk together the soy sauce, brown sugar, garlic, ginger, and cornstarch, if using. Set aside.

In a large skillet over medium-high heat, warm 2 tablespoons of the sesame oil until just smoking. Add the beef and cook, stirring occasionally, until the meat is just about cooked through. Transfer to a plate and set aside. Add the remaining 1 tablespoon of oil to the skillet, then add the onions and cook until they are softened, about 8 minutes. Add the blanched and drained broccoli and cook for 1 minute. Then add the reserved garlic sauce and stir to coat. Return the beef to the skillet and continue to cook until the beef is cooked through and the sauce has reduced slightly, about 3 minutes more. Transfer to serving plates over rice. Sprinkle with sesame seeds and scallions.

*Serves 4*

# Greek Chicken Trough

*There was a moment a few months ago when I was buying feta (the good kind that comes in sheets, rather than that pre-crumbled stuff that doesn't have nearly as much flavor) in bulk. I was just on this major feta bender, looking to toss it into pretty much everything. But this salad is what I found myself making over and over again, sometimes as often as three-plus nights a week. And while really good-quality feta makes this super special, it's the vinaigrette that really makes it shine.*

---

### Ingredients

**For the Greek salad**

1 clove garlic, minced

3 tablespoons olive oil

3 tablespoons red wine vinegar

1 teaspoon dried oregano

Kosher salt and freshly cracked black pepper

2 cups (360 g) roughly chopped ripe tomatoes (I used cherry tomatoes)

2 cups (170 g) roughly chopped cucumbers (I used Persian cucumbers)

2 red or yellow bell peppers, cut into chunks

½ red onion, thinly sliced

1 (8-ounce/225 g) package feta, drained

2 to 3 cups (40 to 60 g) baby arugula

**For the chicken**

1 pound (455 g) boneless chicken breasts, cut into 1-inch (2.5 cm) cubes

Kosher salt and freshly cracked black pepper

1 tablespoon olive oil

2 tablespoons Greek seasoning

**To make the salad:** In a large bowl, whisk together the garlic, olive oil, vinegar, and oregano. Season the vinaigrette with salt and pepper. In the same bowl, combine the tomatoes, cucumbers, bell peppers, and red onion, but don't toss yet. Crumble the feta over the vegetables and top with the arugula. Set aside.

**To make the chicken:** Sprinkle the cubes of chicken breast with salt and pepper. Heat the oil in a nonstick pan over high heat. Add the chicken and sprinkle with the Greek seasoning. Cook the chicken for about 10 minutes, turning every few minutes, until there's a golden crust on all sides.

Add the hot chicken to the salad to wilt the arugula just slightly. Toss to combine. Taste and adjust the salt and pepper as needed. Serve in a big glass bowl and saddle up to the couch.

*Serves 4 to 6*

# Don Antonio's Carne Asada Super Burrito

*If you know, you know. And if you don't, then suffice it to say that Don Antonio's is one of the best Mexican restaurants in LA, and we frequent it regularly. Without fail, we order the same thing over and over again: It's all about the Carne Asada Super Burrito, which is loaded with cheese, carne asada, beans, lettuce, and guac . . . then smothered with enchilada sauce and more cheese. It's the size of a small child but Thomas can easily put it down, and you guessed it, so can I!*

## Ingredients

4 cloves garlic, roughly chopped

1 jalapeño chile, roughly chopped

1 cup (40 g) roughly chopped fresh cilantro

Juice of 2 limes

Juice of 1 orange

½ cup (120 ml) olive oil

Kosher salt and freshly cracked black pepper

1 pound (455 g) flank steak

4 large flour tortillas

1 cup (240 g) refried beans, warmed

2 cups (110 g) shredded romaine lettuce

Gaby's Famous Guacamole (page 257)

2 cups (230 g) freshly grated Colby Jack cheese

3 cups (750 g) store-bought enchilada sauce

In a medium bowl, whisk together the garlic, jalapeño, cilantro, lime juice, orange juice, and olive oil and season with salt and pepper. Place the flank steak in a large baking dish, cover it with the marinade, and refrigerate for 4 to 5 hours. Heat an outdoor grill or a grill pan over high heat and grill the flank steak for 5 minutes on each side. Remove from the grill and let rest before cutting. Cut against the grain into small cubes.

Preheat the broiler. To assemble the burritos, lay out the 4 tortillas on a clean surface. Place equal amounts of beans down the center of each tortilla, leaving room at the ends. Top with equal amounts of shredded lettuce, guacamole, and carne asada. Top each burrito with ¼ cup (35 g) of the shredded cheese. Wrap each burrito up and place them on a baking sheet. Top each burrito with equal amounts of the enchilada sauce and equal amounts of the remaining cheese. Place under the broiler for 3 to 5 minutes, until the cheese melts. Serve immediately.

*Makes 4*

# Grilled Thai Chicken Lettuce Wraps

*Instead of exchanging gifts for the holidays, Thomas and I like to take ourselves on a little vacay instead. During last year's trip, we were lucky enough to eat at a chef's counter where we were at the mercy of whatever he wanted to make. A night with no decisions? Yes, please! One of the MANY courses that came out was a Thai chicken lettuce wrap that blew our minds. It was perfectly seasoned meat wrapped in crisp lettuce with crunchy nuts sprinkled over the top. It was a legit flavor explosion that is easy enough to recreate at home and Thomas and I are both here for it.*

---

## Ingredients

1½ pounds (680 g) boneless skinless chicken thighs, cut into 1-inch (2.5 cm) pieces

Kosher salt and freshly cracked black pepper

⅓ cup (75 ml) sweet chili sauce (from Thai Kitchen, for example)

3 tablespoons reduced-sodium soy sauce

4 cloves garlic, minced

1 tablespoon grated fresh ginger

1 tablespoon minced lemongrass

2 tablespoons fish sauce (optional)

1 tablespoon sriracha, or more to taste

2 tablespoons sesame oil

2 scallions, sliced

Butter lettuce leaves

¼ cup (40 g) toasted peanuts, chopped

Fresh cilantro leaves

Fresh Thai basil leaves

Lime wedges

Season the chicken generously with salt and pepper. In a small bowl, combine the chili sauce, soy sauce, garlic, ginger, lemongrass, fish sauce, if using, and sriracha. Warm the sesame oil in a skillet over medium-high heat. Add the chicken and cook until the thighs are seared well and cooked through, about 10 minutes. Reduce the heat to low and add the sauce. Stir to coat, add the scallions, and continue to cook for another 3 minutes, or until the scallions are wilted and the sauce thickens slightly. To serve, spoon about ¼ cup (115 g) chicken into each lettuce cup. Top with the peanuts, cilantro, and basil and serve wedges of lime alongside.

*Serves 4*

# Curried Turkey Meatballs
## *with Raita*

*There was much debate about this recipe between Thomas and me when I was first developing it—sun-dried tomatoes in a curried meatball? I was skeptical, but Thomas was quick to remind me that I add them to my burgers on the regular to keep them extra juicy. And, as much as I hate to admit it, he was right! The sun-dried tomatoes make these meatballs extra-flavorful, keep them from drying out, and add even more depth of flavor. Whip up a batch and dunk them in the raita . . . it's the perfect casual meal.*

---

### Ingredients

**For the raita**

1 cup (240 ml) full-fat Greek yogurt

1 Persian cucumber, finely diced

1 tablespoon chopped fresh cilantro

Juice of 1 lemon

2 scallions, thinly sliced

¼ teaspoon ground cumin

¼ teaspoon ground coriander

Kosher salt

**For the curried turkey meatballs**

1 pound (455 g) ground turkey or chicken

4 cloves garlic, minced

3 scallions, thinly sliced

¼ cup (30 g) chopped sun-dried tomatoes in olive oil

1 tablespoon minced fresh ginger

1½ tablespoons chopped fresh cilantro

2½ teaspoons curry powder

1 teaspoon kosher salt

½ teaspoon freshly cracked black pepper

2 tablespoons olive oil

**To make the raita:** Put all the ingredients for the raita in a serving bowl and stir to combine. Set aside for 1 hour to allow the flavors to develop while you make the meatballs.

**To make the curried turkey meatballs:** In a large bowl, combine the chicken, garlic, scallions, sun-dried tomatoes, ginger, cilantro, curry powder, salt, and pepper and mix together with a fork or your hands until the ingredients are evenly distributed.

Form the chicken mixture into small meatballs, a little smaller than a golf ball, then pat the top of each one to flatten them out a bit. Heat the olive oil in a large heavy-bottom skillet over medium-high heat. Once the oil is hot, add half of the meatballs and sauté them for 3 to 4 minutes, turning every so often until the outsides are brown, and then continue cooking for about 6 minutes, until the meatballs are cooked through. Remove the first batch from the oil and repeat the process with the remaining meatballs. Serve with the raita for dipping.

*Serves 2 as an entrée, 4 as an appetizer*

# Sweet Potato–
# Black Bean Tacos

*If there's one thing Thomas learned how to do on my last book tour, it was how to prep and cook vegetables. (Okay, that's two things, but they go hand in hand!) The guy goes through a LOT of food on a weekly basis, and without me there to make it for him, he took it upon himself to figure out how to do some advance work in the kitchen so that when it was time to eat, all he had to do was throw together some cooked veg with other ingredients. One of his new tricks is roasting sweet potatoes, which he can then turn into any number of dishes. But our favorite is when we add taco seasoning and black beans to them, stuff it all into tortillas, and top the tacos with avocado and cheese.*

---

### Ingredients

3 tablespoons olive oil

1 large orange sweet potato, cut into ½-inch (12 mm) dice

1 red onion, cut into ½-inch (12 mm) dice

Kosher salt and freshly cracked black pepper

1½ tablespoons taco seasoning

1 (15-ounce/430 g) can black beans, rinsed and drained

8 small flour tortillas

2 ripe avocados, pitted, peeled, and quartered

2 limes, plus more for serving

1 cup (115 g) shredded Monterey Jack cheese

¼ cup (10 g) chopped fresh cilantro

Chipotle Salsa (page 252)

Heat a cast-iron skillet over medium-high heat. Add the olive oil. Once hot, add the sweet potato and red onion and season them with salt and pepper. Sauté for 10 minutes, or until the sweet potatoes start to turn golden brown and the onion becomes translucent. Reduce the heat to medium and stir in the taco seasoning. Continue to cook for 10 minutes more, or until the mixture is fragrant and the sweet potatoes are caramelized and cooked through. Add the black beans, season everything with salt and pepper, and toss to combine. Remove from the heat and set aside.

Over an open flame, char each tortilla for 10 to 15 seconds per side and remove to a clean flat surface. Smash one-fourth of an avocado on top of each tortilla, followed by a large spoonful of the sweet potato and bean mixture. Squeeze lime juice on top of each taco, followed by the cheese and then the cilantro and a bit of salsa. Serve extra lime wedges alongside.

*Serves 4*

# Chicken Taco-Stuffed Bell Peppers

*Give him a recipe and Thomas can find a way to turn it into a taco. (Is there a better meal?) But I figured out how to flip it—taking the flavors of a taco, fixings and all, and turning them into a stuffed-pepper dish that feels a little heartier and healthier. I love this with ground chicken, but you could use any other ground meat.*

---

### Ingredients

1 cup (170 g) multicolored quinoa

4 large bell peppers, halved (from top to bottom), seeds removed

2 teaspoons olive oil, plus more for brushing

1 yellow onion, chopped

8 ounces (225 g) ground chicken or ground turkey, pork, or beef

Kosher salt and freshly cracked black pepper

1 teaspoon ground cumin

1 teaspoon chili powder

1 teaspoon garlic powder

1 (15-ounce/430 g) can black beans, drained

2 cups (230 g) shredded pepper Jack cheese, plus 1 cup (115 g) for topping

¾ cup (about 195 g) Chipotle Salsa (page 252)

4 scallions, thinly sliced

### For the toppings

Gaby's Famous Guacamole (page 257)

Sour cream

Sliced green onions, cilantro leaves, and finely chopped red onions

Cook the quinoa according to the package directions.

Preheat the oven to 375°F (190°C) and lightly grease a 9 by 13-inch (23 by 33 cm) baking dish or rimmed baking sheet. Brush the halved peppers with olive oil and place them cut side up on the baking sheet. Heat the olive oil in a large skillet over medium-high heat. Add the onion and sauté for 5 minutes. Add the chicken and season it with salt and pepper. Cook for 6 to 7 minutes, breaking up the ground meat with the back of a wooden spoon. Add the cumin, chili powder, and garlic powder and stir to combine. Continue to cook until the chicken is fully cooked then remove the pan from the heat. Stir the chicken mixture into the quinoa. Add the black beans, cheese, salsa, and scallions and stir to combine. Taste and adjust the salt and pepper as needed.

Generously stuff the halved peppers with the chicken-quinoa mixture until all the peppers are full, then cover the dish with aluminum foil.

Bake for 30 minutes, covered, then remove the foil, sprinkle a little extra cheese on top of the peppers, increase the heat to 400°F (205°C), and bake for another 15 minutes, or until the peppers are soft and slightly golden brown. Garnish with the assorted toppings.

*Serves 4*

# Kitchen Sink Quesadilla

*There's a stall at one of our favorite farmers' markets that makes a loaded veggie quesadilla, and Thomas and I hit it up pretty much every weekend. They sauté a ton of different veggies, stuff them into an extra-cheesy quesadilla, and grill it until it's crispy. Um, perfection. So you can imagine how pumped I was one night when Thomas offered to make dinner and whipped up his version, which was every bit as gooey and delicious as the original. Below are his favorite vegetables to use, but this will work with just about anything in your fridge.*

---

### Ingredients

1 head baby bok choy, ends trimmed and sliced into ½-inch (12 mm) pieces

5 leaves kale, any variety, sliced into ½-inch (12 mm) ribbons (about 1 packed cup/65 g)

¼ cup (25 g) thinly sliced scallions

1 small carrot, peeled and thinly sliced

1 medium sweet potato, cut into small dice

2 tablespoons olive oil

Kosher salt and freshly cracked black pepper

½ teaspoon red pepper flakes

4 large flour tortillas

4 cups (460 g) shredded Colby Jack or Monterey Jack cheese

Chipotle Salsa (page 252)

Gaby's Famous Guacamole (page 257)

Slice and dice all the vegetables so you're ready to go.

Heat the olive oil in a cast-iron skillet over medium-high heat. Add the sweet potatoes and season them with salt, black pepper, and the red pepper flakes. Sauté the sweet potatoes for about 5 minutes, until they start to soften and slightly char. Add the rest of the vegetables and continue to sauté until the carrots are soft and the kale has wilted, adding a little water if the mixture is looking dry. Season everything with salt and pepper to taste and remove from the heat.

Either free up the cast-iron skillet by removing the vegetables to a medium bowl, or put another cast-iron skillet on the stove. Place 1 tortilla at a time into the skillet. Sprinkle 1 cup (115 g) of the shredded cheese on the tortilla. Spoon ½ to ¾ cup (75 to 115 g) of the vegetable mixture on top of the cheese and turn the heat to medium. Allow the cheese to melt for about 1 minute and then fold the tortilla in half. Continue to cook the quesadilla until one side is golden brown and then flip and cook until the other side is equally golden. Remove the quesadilla from the pan and cut it into thirds. Repeat with the remaining tortillas and fillings. Serve with salsa and guacamole.

*Serves 4*

# Chapter 7
# Sides: The Best Part of Any Meal

To me, it doesn't get better than side dishes. I love how you can mix and match them with your mains, or just combine them to make a meal. Most of the time when I'm going out to eat, I'd rather just order one main dish and then ALL THE SIDES, especially ones that center around vegetables. The same goes for when I'm cooking for people—I like to make lots of small veg-forward plates to keep things interesting and tasty, while also keeping the meal from feeling too heavy. In my opinion, the key to a great side dish is to let the vegetables shine. That means learning how to cook them properly (something I'll cover in this chapter!), and how to season them just enough to bring out their natural flavor. Stick with me, and your side dish game will forever be changed.

# *Cacio e Pepe* Asparagus

*Ever since coming back from my birthday trip to Italy a few years ago, I've basically been turning everything into cacio e pepe, an addicting mix of olive oil, Parmesan, and black pepper. Pasta is the usual base for this recipe but veggies . . . whole different ball game. I love giving asparagus this treatment, but you could do this with just about any veggie. Picky eaters rejoice!*

## Ingredients

2 pounds (910 g) asparagus, ends trimmed

2 tablespoons olive oil

½ teaspoon kosher salt

½ teaspoon freshly cracked black pepper

⅓ cup (30 g) shredded Parmesan cheese

Juice of 1 lemon

Preheat the oven to 425°F (220°C). Lay the asparagus spears on a baking sheet, drizzle with the olive oil, and sprinkle with the salt and pepper. Scatter the cheese on top and roast for about 15 minutes, until just tender. Remove the pan from the oven and drizzle with the lemon juice. Transfer the asparagus to a platter and serve.

*Serves 6 to 8*

# *Cauliflower* Shawarma

*Cauliflower is the perfect canvas for spicing things up, which makes it the ultimate pairing with a shawarma spice blend. I roast the cauliflower until it's caramelized, golden, and meaty—perfect for a side dish or layering with other Middle Eastern flavors in a bowl (page 146).*

---

## Ingredients

2 pounds (910 g) cauliflower florets

1 tablespoon ground turmeric

1 tablespoon ground cumin

1 teaspoon kosher salt

1 teaspoon freshly cracked black pepper

1 teaspoon ground coriander

1 teaspoon paprika

¼ cup (60 ml) olive oil

Fresh lemon juice

Preheat the oven to 425°F (220°C).

Clean and dry the cauliflower florets and transfer them to a parchment-lined baking sheet. In a medium bowl, combine the turmeric, cumin, salt, pepper, coriander, paprika, and olive oil and stir to blend. Drizzle the spiced oil on top of the cauliflower and toss to combine so the florets are evenly coated. Roast for 35 minutes, or until the cauliflower is caramelized and browned. Remove from the oven and serve as needed with a squeeze of lemon juice.

*Serves 4 to 6*

# Cheesy Lemon
# Brussels Sprouts

*It's not normal for us to have any leftover cheese in our house, but one day I had to clean out the fridge before a big dinner party, and throwing anything out—especially cheese—was out of the question. I decided I would just dump extra cheese over everything, and this dish was born. It's like the brussels died and went to mac 'n' cheese heaven.*

---

### Ingredients

2 pounds (910 g) brussels sprouts, trimmed and halved or quartered, depending on size

¼ cup (60 ml) olive oil

Kosher salt and freshly cracked black pepper

1 teaspoon red pepper flakes

1 cup (110 g) shredded fresh mozzarella cheese

1 cup (110 g) grated Gruyère cheese

1 lemon

Preheat the oven to 425°F (220°C).

Place the halved brussels sprouts on a parchment-lined baking sheet. Drizzle with the olive oil and season with salt, pepper and the red pepper flakes. Roast for 30 to 35 minutes, until the sprouts are fully cooked and the edges are crispy.

Remove from the oven and sprinkle the mozzarella and Gruyère on top. Return the pan to the oven and roast for an additional 5 minutes, or until the cheese is fully melted.

Remove the pan from the oven, squeeze the lemon juice on top of the roasted brussels sprouts, and adjust the salt and pepper as needed. Serve immediately.

*Serves 6 to 8*

# *Asian* Long Beans

*Guidelines to success: 1) These need to be eaten hot. 2) If you can find long beans (usually available in Asian markets), use those. 3) If not, haricots vert work great. 4) Did I mention these are best served hot? I know a lot of my recipes can be served at any temperature, but these need to be straight off the stovetop for maximum impact.* **Note:** *You can adjust the quantity of sambal depending on how spicy you want to go—1 tablespoon is pretty mild while 1½ to 2 tablespoons will pack a punch.*

---

## Ingredients

2 tablespoons grapeseed oil or other high-heat oil

1½ pounds (680 g) long beans, ends trimmed and cut in half, about 6 to 8 inches (15 to 20 cm) long

1 tablespoon soy sauce

1 to 2 tablespoons sambal

6 cloves garlic, minced

¼ cup (25 g) sliced scallions

Freshly cracked black pepper

Sesame seeds (optional)

Heat the oil in a large skillet over high heat. Once the oil shimmers, add the green beans and sauté, stirring frequently, for 10 to 12 minutes, until the beans are charred.

In a small bowl, stir together the soy sauce, sambal, garlic, and 2 tablespoons water. Reduce the heat to low, add the sauce to the green beans, and stir together for 1 minute. Remove the pan from the heat. Add the scallions and toss to combine. Season with pepper if needed and garnish with sesame seeds if desired. Transfer to a platter and serve hot.

*Serves 6 to 8*

# Omi's
# Fried Potatoes

*If you made Omi's Green Beans from my second cookbook, then you know my Omi is a boss. She just gets it when it comes to cooking simple yet flavor-packed food, and these potatoes are no different. We used to BEG her to make them when we were kids and would fight to see who got the crispiest bits and all the jammy, caramelized onions. Now that I can make these for myself, I've also realized that the best part about this recipe is that the simpler you keep things, the better they'll be. No need to par-boil the potatoes first—Omi and I agree that they fall apart too easily—and no need to peel the potatoes if you're using Yukon Golds. That said, you do need to babysit these as they cook—they need a lot of stirring for maximum crispness.*

---

### Ingredients

2 tablespoons olive oil

1 large Vidalia onion, cut into large chunks

1 pound (455 g) baby Yukon Gold potatoes, sliced in ⅓-inch (8 mm) rounds

Kosher salt and freshly cracked black pepper

Fresh chives, snipped

1 lemon, cut in half

In a large cast-iron skillet, heat the oil over medium heat. Add the onion and sauté for 3 to 4 minutes, until fragrant. Add the potatoes and stir to combine. Continue to cook, stirring every few minutes, until the onions are fully cooked, 15 to 20 minutes. Some of the chunks of onion will fall apart—that's good, you want the crispy bits. Season with salt and pepper. Once the potatoes are fork tender, remove the pan from the heat and garnish with chives and the juice of half a lemon to start. Taste and adjust the lemon juice, if needed, or add more salt. Serve immediately.

*Serves 2 to 4*

# *Roasted*
# Beets and Labneh

*I know so many of you love sweet, earthy beets but pass them up for other root veggies because they can be kind of a pain to make. But did you know that you don't have to peel beets before roasting them? And that if you buy an orange variety instead of red, they don't stain your hands? Game changer! (For the record, I like a mix of orange and red because of how pretty it looks on the plate.) If you're still not convinced that you can make beets taste amazing at home, know that it really doesn't take much more than adding a dollop of labneh, a thick yogurt you can find in most specialty markets. Plain Greek yogurt strained through a cheesecloth for a few hours will do the trick too. Season it with some salt and pepper, add your favorite fresh-herb vinaigrette, and you're good to go.*

---

### Ingredients

4 bunches beets, roughly 12 total (half orange, half red)

2 shallots, peeled and sliced into quarters

¼ cup (60 ml) olive oil

1 teaspoon red pepper flakes

Kosher salt and freshly cracked black pepper

2 cups (480 ml) labneh (thick Greek yogurt)

2 to 3 tablespoons Basil Vinaigrette (page 254)

1 to 2 ripe avocados, pitted, peeled, and sliced into wedges or chunks

Fresh mint leaves

Fresh dill sprigs

Maldon sea salt

Preheat the oven to 425°F (220°C). Line a baking sheet with parchment paper.

Scrub and trim the beets and slice them into wedges. Toss the beets and shallots with the olive oil and season with the red pepper flakes, salt, and pepper. Transfer the seasoned beets and shallots to the prepared baking sheet and roast for 40 to 50 minutes, until fork tender. Remove from the oven and set aside to come to room temp.

Spread the labneh on a large platter, dollop with basil vinaigrette, and scatter with the beets and avocado wedges. Sprinkle with fresh mint leaves, dill, and flaky salt and serve.

*Serves 6 to 8*

# Host a Taco Night

This menu is an ode to one of my obsessions: carnitas tacos. It's my go-to dish for entertaining, and I've perfected the art of making it a total showstopper because for this bad boy, we're going bone-in WHOLE PORK BUTT, bo ssam style (hat tip to David Chang and Momofuku for forever changing my bo ssam game by inventing the perfect slow-roasting method versus the traditional boiling). These dishes are like a master class in how to make a perfectly balanced meal—not too indulgent, not too skimpy. The key is using lots of big, bold, and bright flavors that play well together, pairing them with tons of seasonal fruits and veg, and topping it off with a refreshing cocktail or two.

---

Carnitas

Homemade Smoky Pinto Beans

Spicy Mexican Fruit Salad

Green Rice

Homemade Tortilla Chips

Palomas

Cucumber Margaritas

*Serves 6 to 8*

# Carnitas

**Ingredients**

1 whole bone-in pork butt (8 to 10 pounds/3.6 to 4.5 kg)

1 cup (200 g) sugar

½ cup (65 g) plus 1 teaspoon kosher salt

1 tablespoon chili powder

1½ teaspoons ground cumin

½ teaspoon garlic powder

½ teaspoon red pepper flakes

½ teaspoon dried oregano

½ teaspoon paprika

½ teaspoon freshly cracked black pepper

2 limes

2 oranges

**For serving**

Butter lettuce cups

Charred flour and corn tortillas

Chipotle Salsa (page 252)

Gaby's Famous Guacamole (page 257)

Pico de Gallo (page 257)

Pickled Onions (page 256)

Pickled jalapeños, chopped white onions, cilantro, scallions, and lime wedges in individual bowls

Place the pork in a large, shallow bowl. Mix together the sugar and ½ cup (65 g) of the salt in another bowl, then rub the sugar-and-salt mixture all over the meat. Cover the pork with plastic wrap and place in the refrigerator for at least 6 hours or overnight.

When you're ready to cook, preheat the oven to 300°F (150°C). Remove the pork from the refrigerator and brush off the sugar-and-salt mixture. Score the fat cap of the pork butt in a crosshatch pattern, place the pork in a roasting pan, fat side up, and roast for approximately 7 to 8 hours.

After the first hour, baste hourly with the pan juices. After an additional 5 hours, remove the meat from the oven. Stir together the chili powder, cumin, garlic powder, red pepper flakes, oregano, paprika, the remaining 1 teaspoon salt, and the black pepper and sprinkle the spice mix over the top of the roast. Place the pork back in the oven and let it cook for another hour or so. If the spices start to burn, tent the pork with aluminum foil. The meat is done when it's super easy to tear apart with a fork. It should basically collapse when you try to pull it apart.

To create a crust, turn up the oven to 500°F (260°C) and juice the limes and oranges over the pork. Roast the pork butt for another 10 to 15 minutes, until a dark caramel crust develops on the meat.

Serve hot, with the accoutrements. Invite diners to create lettuce wraps with pieces of the pork and whatever toppings they desire.

# Homemade Smoky Pinto Beans

## Ingredients

2 tablespoons olive oil

1 yellow onion, finely diced

6 cloves garlic, roughly chopped

1 chicken or vegetable bouillon cube

1 bay leaf

1 chipotle pepper in adobo, roughly chopped

1 (4-ounce/115 g) can diced green chiles

1½ teaspoons ground cumin

1½ teaspoons chili powder

1 pound (455 g) dry pinto beans

1 teaspoon kosher salt

Juice of 1 lime

**To make the beans in an Instant Pot:**
Turn the Instant Pot to sauté. Add the oil, onion, and garlic and sauté for 3 to 4 minutes. Add the bouillon cube, bay leaf, chipotle pepper, green chiles, cumin, and chili powder and stir to combine. Add the dry beans, salt, and 4 cups (960 ml) water and give the mixture a stir. Cover with the lid and turn the vent at the top to the "sealed" position. Set the Instant Pot to cook for 48 minutes on the "chili" setting.

When the timer goes off, let the steam pressure naturally release for at least 20 minutes before attempting to remove the lid. There shouldn't be too much liquid remaining—if there is, remove some carefully with a ladle. Smash the beans until they are half smashed and half whole. Adjust the salt as needed and stir in the lime juice.

**To make the beans on the stovetop:** Soak the dry beans in water overnight. When ready to cook, drain and discard the soaking liquid.

Heat the oil in a large skillet over medium-high heat. Add the onion and garlic and sauté for 3 to 4 minutes. Add the bouillon cube, bay leaf, chipotle pepper, green chiles, cumin, and chili powder and stir to combine. Add the soaked beans, salt, and 4 cups (960 ml) water, cover with the lid, and cook for 35 to 40 minutes, until the beans are fork tender.

The beans should have absorbed most of the water—if there is more than ½ cup (120 ml) remaining, remove some carefully with a ladle. Smash the beans until they are half smashed and half whole. Adjust the salt as needed and stir in the lime juice.

Chapter 8

# If At First You Don't Succeed, Have Dessert

I'm not a fancy dessert person—it's just not who I am.
I'd much rather have something that's simple, but every
bit as gooey, chewy, and decadent (plus bonus points for
chocolatey) as any complicated pastry could be. So that's
what this chapter is all about: cookies, cobblers, bars,
and crisps that are easy to make and even easier to eat.
Fair warning: It will take all of your willpower to save any for
sharing. I speak from experience! But when it's homemade,
I say any guilt about overindulging belongs in the same
category as a plate: not required.

# Texas
# Sheet Cake

*This is my family's go to cake! It's the one we all wanted as our birthday cake. 1) It's delicious. 2) It's huge (see: Texas). 3) It absolutely doubles as breakfast. It's just one of those really straightforward dessert recipes that you can't mess up. And a hot tip from my mom: If you don't have buttermilk on hand, you can use regular milk, yogurt, or kefir instead.*

---

### Ingredients

**For the cake**
2 cups (400 g) granulated sugar
2 cups (250 g) all-purpose flour
1 teaspoon baking soda
½ cup (115 g/1 stick) unsalted butter
¼ cup (25 g) unsweetened cocoa powder
½ cup (120 ml) buttermilk
2 large eggs
1 teaspoon vanilla extract

**For the icing**
½ cup (115 g/1 stick) unsalted butter
¼ cup (25 g) unsweetened cocoa powder
6 tablespoons (90 ml) milk
1 pound (455 g) powdered sugar
1 teaspoon vanilla extract

Preheat the oven to 400°F (205°C).

**To make the cake:** Put the granulated sugar, flour, and baking soda in a large bowl and stir to combine. Set aside.

In a small saucepan, combine the butter, cocoa powder, and 1 cup (240 ml) water and bring to a boil. Once the butter-cocoa mixture is boiling, remove from the heat, carefully pour into the dry ingredients, and stir to combine. The batter will be very thick.

Whisk together the buttermilk, eggs, and vanilla, add to the batter, and stir to combine.

Transfer the batter to an 18 by 13-inch (46 by 33 cm) sheet pan and bake for 15 minutes. The cake should be spongy.

**To make the icing:** While the sheet cake is baking, put the butter, cocoa powder, and milk in a saucepan over medium heat and stir to combine. Add the powered sugar and vanilla and stir until super smooth. Pour the icing over the cake and let it set before slicing and serving.

*Serves 12+*

# Every Damn Day
# Chocolate Chip Cookies

*I've made hundreds of cookies over the course of my life, and while many (many) of them were pretty amazing, this one wins in every way. The ratios are all spot-on, the chocolate is plentiful, and the cookies are chewy and dense.* **Note:** *Don't forget to tap the pan on the counter after baking the cookies—it's a tip I learned in pastry school one million years ago and it's still the best way to get out all the air bubbles from the dough, making for even denser, chewier cookies.*

---

## Ingredients

1 cup (225 g/2 sticks) unsalted butter, at room temperature

1½ cups (330 g) packed brown sugar

½ cup (100 g) granulated sugar

2 large eggs

2 teaspoons vanilla extract

2½ cups (315 g) all-purpose flour

1 teaspoon kosher salt

1 teaspoon baking soda

1 teaspoon baking powder

1 cup (175 g) semisweet chocolate chips

1 cup (175 g) semisweet chocolate disks

Maldon sea salt

Combine the butter and sugars in a stand mixer and mix until smooth and pale yellow, about 3 minutes.

Add the eggs and vanilla and continue to mix, making sure to scrape down the sides of the bowl with a spatula.

Add the flour, kosher salt, baking soda, and baking powder and mix on low speed until everything is just combined. Stir in the chocolate chips and disks by hand. Cover the dough with plastic wrap and refrigerate for 2 to 72 hours. Preheat the oven to 350°F (175°C). Line a baking sheet with parchment paper.

Scoop out 2 tablespoons of the dough and roll into a ball. Place the dough onto the prepared pan, 12 cookies per sheet, and sprinkle each with a pinch of Maldon sea salt. Bake for 10 to 12 minutes, until the edges are just slightly golden brown and the center is still a bit soft.

Remove the baking sheet from the oven and carefully slam the sheet onto a flat surface to release any air in the cookies. Then, let the cookies rest for about 5 minutes before transferring them from the baking sheet onto a cooling rack. Repeat this process with the remaining dough. Enjoy responsibly.

Store in an airtight container the fridge for 2 weeks, or in the freezer forever. But let's be honest, they never last that long.

*Makes roughly 3 dozen cookies*

# Strawberry Crispy
# Cobbler

*Not quite a crisp, not quite a cobbler—it's just freakin' fantastic.*
*Serve with ice cream. Done.*

---

## Ingredients

### For the biscuits

¼ cup (55 g) packed brown sugar

1 tablespoon baking powder

2 teaspoons finely grated lemon zest

1 teaspoon kosher salt

2 cups (250 g) all-purpose flour, plus more for surface

¾ cup (65 g) old-fashioned oats

½ cup (115 g/1 stick) chilled unsalted butter, cut into small pieces

1⅓ cups (315 ml) chilled heavy cream

### For the filling

2 pounds (910 g) pitted and hulled strawberries

½ cup (100 g) granulated sugar

2 tablespoons fresh lemon juice

2 tablespoons cornstarch

1 teaspoon vanilla extract

½ teaspoon almond extract

½ teaspoon kosher salt

2 tablespoons unsalted butter, melted

2 tablespoons raw sugar

Vanilla ice cream

Preheat the oven to 400°F (205°C). Line a baking sheet with aluminum foil.

**To make the biscuits:** Combine the brown sugar, baking powder, lemon zest, salt, flour, and oats in a large bowl. Add the butter and use a fork or pastry cutter to smash the butter into the flour mixture until the butter is combined and pieces are no larger than a pea.

Slowly pour the heavy cream into the bowl, mixing it into the flour mixture with a fork as you pour. Use a heavy-duty spatula or your hands to incorporate the dough into one large mass. It will be a little wet, that's fine. Break off roughly golf ball–size pieces of dough and roll them into balls. Transfer the balls to a plate and chill until ready to use.

**To make the filling:** In a large bowl, combine the strawberries, granulated sugar, lemon juice, cornstarch, vanilla extract, almond extract, and salt and toss to coat. Transfer the filling into a round 9-inch (23 cm) ceramic baking pan with 2-inch (5 cm) sides and gently press down on the mixture to pack it into place.

Place the baking dish on the prepared baking sheet and arrange the chilled biscuits over the filling—they should pretty much cover the top. Brush the tops of the biscuits with the melted butter and sprinkle with the raw sugar.

Bake for 10 minutes. Reduce the heat to 350°F (175°C) and continue to bake until the biscuits are golden brown and the juices are bubbling, 50 to 65 minutes more. Let cool slightly. Serve the crispy cobbler with ice cream.

*Serves 8 to 10*

# Caramel, Marshmallow, Chocolate Chunk Brownies

*We all know Ben & Jerry's Phish Food ice cream, right? Well it's my favorite store-bought flavor of all time. BUT, I keep asking them to add brownie batter into the mix and no one has responded to my requests! So I took it upon myself to come up with a recipe that takes all the best parts of Phish Food and turns them into brownies. Don't even bother trying to cut these, just grab some spoons and attack. And Ben & Jerry, if you're reading this, I'm available for flavor consulting any time!*

---

## Ingredients

10 ounces (280 g) caramels, peeled

½ cup (120 ml) evaporated milk

10 tablespoons (145 g) unsalted butter, at room temperature

1¼ cups (250 g) sugar

¾ cup (70 g) unsweetened cocoa powder

½ teaspoon kosher salt

1 teaspoon vanilla paste, or 2 teaspoons vanilla extract

2 large eggs

½ cup (65 g) all-purpose flour

½ cup (85 g) semisweet chocolate chips

1 cup (50 g) mini marshmallows

In a small pot, combine the peeled caramels and evaporated milk. Heat over medium heat, stirring with a wooden spoon until all the caramels are melted. Remove from the heat.

Preheat the oven to 350°F (175°C). Spray a 10-inch (25 cm) cast-iron skillet or a 9 by 9-inch (23 cm) baking pan with nonstick cooking spray.

In a pot over medium heat, combine the butter, sugar, cocoa powder, and salt and mix with a whisk for 2 minutes. Remove from the heat and mix in the vanilla and eggs. Stir in the flour, chocolate chips, and marshmallows, and set aside.

Pour half of the brownie batter into the prepared pan and bake for 10 minutes. Remove the pan from the oven, pour the caramel sauce over the cooked brownies, then add the remaining brownie batter on top of the caramel. Using a butter knife, swirl the top two layers together. Return to the oven and bake for 20 minutes.

Let the brownies cool to room temperature before transferring the pan to the refrigerator to chill for at least 1 hour before serving.

*Makes 10-ish brownies*

# Raspberry Frangipane
# Galette

*I'm a big fan of desserts that are easy to whip together and yet really visually impressive. Galettes are just the thing because they sound and look like they took a lot of time and special techniques but are so simple to make. The same goes for frangipane, a sweet almond filling. So fancy sounding, yet so easy and so, so tasty. If you want to make this recipe even easier, you can make the crust in a food processor then store it in the freezer for a last-minute dessert.*

---

## Ingredients

1¼ cups (155 g) all-purpose flour, plus more for sprinkling

3 tablespoons granulated sugar

¼ teaspoon kosher salt

7 tablespoons (100 g) cold unsalted butter, diced into varied sizes

2 to 6 tablespoons (30 to 90 ml) ice cold water

Frangipane (recipe follows)

2 cups (250 g) raspberries

1 large egg white plus 1 teaspoon water, whisked together

Powdered sugar

Whisk together the flour, 2 tablespoons of the granulated sugar, and the salt in a medium bowl. Cut the butter into the flour mixture with a fork, pastry cutter, or clean fingers, rubbing the butter and flour together. You want it to look like coarse meal with some larger flat pieces of butter.

With a mixing spoon start mixing in the ice water, 2 tablespoons at first and then 1 tablespoon at a time until the dough just holds together.

Shape the dough into a flat disk about 5 inches (23 cm) in diameter. Wrap it in plastic wrap and chill in the refrigerator for at least 30 minutes or up to 2 days.

Preheat the oven to 425°F (220°C). Line a baking sheet with parchment paper.

Remove the dough from the fridge and place it on a well-floured board. Sprinkle some flour onto the top of the disk and, using a well-floured rolling pin, roll out the dough from the center in all directions until the disk is about 12 inches (30.5 cm) in diameter. If needed, sprinkle more flour on the top as you roll to keep the pin from sticking.

Continued

Transfer the dough to the prepared baking sheet. With a spoon, spread the frangipane on the dough to form a 9-inch (23 cm) circle, leaving 2 to 3 inches (5 to 7.5 cm) of dough around the edges uncovered. Scatter the raspberries across the frangipane and begin to fold the edges of the dough to cover a little of the filling, gently folding and pleating the dough all the way around.

Brush the crust with the egg wash and sprinkle with the remaining 1 tablespoon of granulated sugar.

Place the galette in the freezer for 15 minutes. Once chilled, bake the galette for 15 minutes. Reduce the oven temperature to 375°F (190°C) and continue baking until the crust is golden brown and the frangipane is puffed and golden, 30 to 40 minutes.

Let cool on the baking sheet for 10 to 20 minutes. Dust with powdered sugar and serve warm or at room temperature.

*Serves 8+*

# Frangipane

5 tablespoons (70 g) unsalted butter, at room temperature

⅓ cup (65 g) plus 1 tablespoon sugar

1 large egg, at room temperature

1 teaspoon vanilla extract

1 teaspoon orange zest

¾ cup (70 g) almond meal

2 tablespoons all-purpose flour

Pinch of salt

In a stand mixer fitted with the paddle attachment, cream the butter and sugar together on medium speed until light and fluffy, about 4 minutes. Reduce the speed to low and mix in the egg; once fully incorporated, mix in the vanilla and orange zest. With the speed still on low, add the almond meal, flour, and salt. Increase the speed to medium and continue to mix until the frangipane is fluffy, about 4 minutes more. Set aside until you're ready to assemble the galette.

# Blackberry Thyme
# Cobbler

*Why have one cobbler in the book when you can have two? Aside from being one of my favorite warm-weather desserts to make with the crazy amounts of fruit I bring home from the market, I wanted to give you the option of making a more traditional cobbler with biscuit topping (as opposed to the crisp-style cobbler on page 231). I also wanted to showcase this unique filling that I came up with after drinking a blackberry-thyme cocktail. I realized that I needed many fresh herbs in my dessert life, and the rest was history.*

---

## Ingredients

### For the filling
7 cups (1 kg) blackberries
¾ cup (150 g) granulated sugar
2 teaspoons minced fresh thyme leaves
2 tablespoons cornstarch
Pinch of kosher salt
Pinch of freshly grated nutmeg
1 tablespoon fresh lemon juice

### For the biscuits
1½ cups (190 g) all-purpose flour
3 tablespoons light brown sugar
1½ teaspoons baking powder
½ teaspoon kosher salt
Zest of ½ lemon
1¼ cups (300 ml) plus 2 tablespoons
   heavy cream
1 tablespoon granulated sugar

Vanilla ice cream or whipped cream

Preheat the oven to 375°F (190°C) and lightly grease a 2-quart (2 L) baking dish.

To make the filling: Wash and dry the berries and place them in a large bowl. Add the sugar, thyme, cornstarch, salt, nutmeg, and lemon juice. Lightly stir to mix and then pour the berry mixture into the prepared pan.

To make the biscuits: In a medium bowl, combine the flour, brown sugar, baking powder, salt, and lemon zest. Stir to mix and break up any clumps of brown sugar. Slowly pour 1¼ cups (300 ml) of the cream into the flour mixture and stir to combine to create wet shaggy dough.

Drop heaping 1 to 2 tablespoon mounds of dough onto the berries, leaving space between the dough to see the berries.

Brush the tops of the dough with the remaining 2 tablespoons heavy cream and sprinkle with the 1 tablespoon of granulated sugar. Bake until the biscuits are golden brown, 50 to 60 minutes.

Let the cobbler cool for 15 minutes. Serve with vanilla ice cream or dollops of fresh whipped cream.

*Serves 8+*

# Chapter 9
# Sauces Make the Meal

One of the biggest reasons people have for not wanting to cook more often is because it's complicated or takes too much time. Welcome, my friends, to the whole wild world of sauces. Keeping an arsenal of homemade condiments in the fridge is one of my favorite tricks of the trade. By tossing together a few simple ingredients—most of which you may already have in your pantry—blending them up, and then keeping them on hand, you are already about 80 percent of the way done with creating a simple and delicious meal. A few examples: Roast some veggies and throw some sauce on them. Boil some pasta and throw some sauce on it. Grill some meat and throw some sauce on it. See where I'm going with this? The right sauce can amp up a meal's flavor with a drizzle or shmear. They're especially great when you're trying to get more vegetables into your life, and almost all of the sauces in this chapter would be great with veg, whether they're roasted, grilled, steamed, or sautéed. The sauces can mostly be frozen too, so you'll never have an excuse to not cook again!

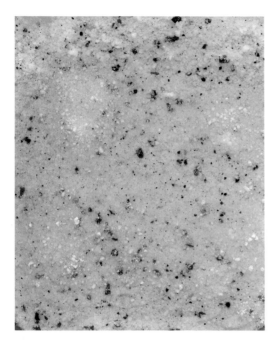

# Creamy Pecorino Vinaigrette

*The latest and greatest in my arsenal of dressings. This creamy Pecorino vinaigrette is excellent over veggies, great in a salad, and so good I sometimes find myself eating it with a spoon. Don't judge me.*

### Ingredients
2 tablespoons fresh lemon juice

½ cup (120 ml) olive oil

4 cloves garlic, minced

½ cup (50 g) grated Pecorino cheese

Kosher salt and freshly cracked black pepper

½ teaspoon red pepper flakes

In a medium bowl, whisk together all the ingredients. Taste and adjust the salt and pepper as needed.

*Makes ½ cup (120 ml)*

# Green Goddess Dip

*Fresh, tangy, and gorgeously green—this one checks all the boxes and is delicious over pretty much anything that you're cooking up or tossing together.*

### Ingredients
2 scallions, white and light green parts only, roughly chopped

1 ripe avocado, pitted and peeled

1 teaspoon lemon zest plus 2 tablespoons fresh lemon juice

1 to 2 tablespoons champagne vinegar

3 to 5 tablespoons (45 to 75 ml) water

¼ cup (60 ml) extra-virgin olive oil

1 cup (40 g) loosely packed chopped fresh basil

⅓ cup (12 g) chopped fresh parsley

¼ cup (11 g) snipped fresh chives

1 clove garlic

Kosher salt and freshly cracked black pepper

Combine everything in a food processor or high-powered blender and blend until smooth. Add a few extra tablespoons of water if you need to smooth it out to dressing consistency. Taste and adjust the salt and pepper as needed. Use immediately, or store in the refrigerator in an airtight container for up to 4 days.

*Makes 1½ cups (360 ml)*

# Garlic Tomato Confit

*I combined my tomato confit and garlic confit to give you the most luscious, jammy, tomato-filled situation to rub all over bread, fold into pasta sauce, slather over meat and veggies, or dollop on a veggie bowl.*

## Ingredients
1 pound (455 g) cherry tomatoes, halved

⅓ cup (75 ml) good-quality olive oil

8 cloves garlic, peeled

Kosher salt and freshly cracked black pepper

In a medium skillet over medium-high heat, combine the tomatoes and olive oil. Add the garlic and a pinch of salt and pepper.

Once the oil starts to heat up and the tomatoes start to blister, reduce the heat to medium-low and let the tomatoes simmer for at least 30 minutes or up to 1 hour, stirring every 10 minutes. The tomatoes should be falling apart. Remove the pan from the heat and allow the confit to cool for at least 20 minutes.

*Makes about 1½ cups (250 g)*

# Whole Roasted Garlic

*If you make a whole head of roasted garlic and don't eat half of it before using it on whatever it was intended for, are you really living your best life? I make this in bulk—as in ten garlic heads at a time—because it's great slathered on anything.*

## Ingredients
1 head of garlic

2 teaspoons olive oil

Preheat the oven to 400°F (205°C).

Trim about ¼ inch (6 mm) off the top of the head of garlic to expose the tops of the garlic cloves. Drizzle the olive oil over the top of the garlic, letting the oil sink down into the cloves.

Wrap the garlic in a piece of aluminum foil and roast on the middle shelf of the oven. Check the garlic after 40 minutes; if it's golden and caramelized, remove. If it's still quite pale, let the garlic roast for another 10 minutes.

Let the garlic cool slightly, and use as needed. Roasted garlic can be refrigerated for up to 2 weeks.

*Makes about ¼ cup (65 g)*

# Lemon Tahini Dressing

*Maybe one of my best creations yet. It's great as a drizzle, perfect for dipping veggies, and doubles as a vegan Caesar salad dressing. Just know that tahini likes to thicken up, so if you store this in the fridge for a few days, you'll want to thin it out with a little more water before using it. But don't worry—it will still retain its flavor.*

### Ingredients
8 ounces (225 g) tahini

Juice of 1 lemon

2 cloves garlic

½ teaspoon kosher salt

½ teaspoon ground cumin

Combine all the ingredients in a food processor or blender and blend until perfectly smooth like a peanut butter. Stream in 1 to 2 cups (240 to 480 ml) water a little bit at a time until your desired consistency is reached. Taste and adjust the salt as needed.

*Makes 2½ cups (600 ml)*

# Chipotle Salsa

*I'm a salsa snob, that's all there is to it. I grew up in Arizona; it's just par for the course. If it's in my kitchen, then it's gotta be good. This chipotle salsa is in the weekly rotation over here at WGC headquarters because it's so easy to whip up and is perfect for anything from tacos and bowls, to chips and guac, to anything else that needs a little punch.*

### Ingredients
1 (28-ounce/795 g) can fire-roasted tomatoes

½ yellow onion, chopped (roughly ½ cup/55 g)

2 cloves garlic

½ jalapeño chile

2 chipotle peppers in adobo, or more if desired, plus 1 teaspoon of the adobo sauce

1 teaspoon kosher salt

½ teaspoon freshly cracked black pepper

½ cup (20 g) chopped fresh cilantro

Juice of 1 lime

Combine all the ingredients in a food processor or high-powered blender and pulse until everything is evenly blended. Taste and adjust the salt and pepper as needed. Add more chipotle peppers if you like it extra spicy. Remove from the food processor or blender and refrigerate until ready to serve.

*Makes 2½ cups (600 ml)*

# Salsa Verde

*This is my go-to sauce for using up all the herbs that I buy on a weekly basis at the farmers' market. It's great spooned over veggies, fish, chicken, and beef . . . or used it as a marinade.*

### Ingredients

1 bunch fresh parsley, stems removed

1 bunch fresh cilantro, stems removed

20 leaves fresh basil

2 cloves garlic

2 tablespoons red wine vinegar

½ to ¾ cup (120 to 180 ml) olive oil

Kosher salt and freshly cracked black pepper

Combine all the ingredients in a food processor or high-powered blender and pulse until everything is evenly blended. Taste and adjust the salt and pepper as needed. Add more chipotle peppers if you like it extra spicy. Remove from the food processor or blender and refrigerate until ready to serve.

*Makes 2½ cups (600 ml)*

# Asian Vinaigrette

*Possibly the most addicting dressing ever—it's so flavorful that even something as simple as a cucumber salad goes to the next level with a sprinkle of this vin. I also love this over a steak salad, tossed with pasta, or added to slaw for an Asian spin.*

### Ingredients

3 tablespoons olive oil

2 tablespoons soy sauce

Juice of ½ lime

½ teaspoon sesame oil

1½ tablespoons rice wine vinegar

1 small shallot, finely diced

1 (1-inch/2.5 cm) piece fresh ginger, finely chopped

2 cloves garlic, finely chopped

½ teaspoon red pepper flakes

Kosher salt

In a medium bowl, whisk together all the ingredients. Taste and adjust the salt as needed.

*Makes ½ cup (120 ml)*

# Pickled Onions

*Keep these in the fridge at all times because you never know when you're going to want to throw them on a burger (page 120) or into tacos (page 185). They keep for weeks in the refrigerator and the longer they sit, the prettier they get!*

### Ingredients

1 cup (240 ml) apple cider vinegar

1 tablespoon sugar

1½ teaspoons kosher salt

1 medium red onion, cut in thin slices

In a small bowl, whisk the apple cider vinegar, sugar, and salt with 1 cup (240 ml) water until the sugar and salt dissolve. Place the sliced onions in a jar; pour the vinegar mixture over the onions. Let sit at room temperature for 1 hour. Drain and serve as needed.

*Makes roughly 1 cup (120 g)*

# Homemade Chunky Garlic Bread Crumbs

*Buying packaged bread crumbs at the store just isn't worth it. These are loaded with so much more flavor, thanks to the combo of both olive oil and butter, plus garlic and salt. Just be warned: You'll be tempted to make a meal out of these on their own.*

### Ingredients

2 tablespoons olive oil

1 tablespoon unsalted butter

4 slices French bread (a few days old), torn into very small pieces (about 1½ cups/250 g)

2 cloves garlic, chopped

½ teaspoon kosher salt

Heat the olive oil and butter in a large nonstick skillet over medium heat. When the butter has melted, add the bread and sauté for 3 to 5 minutes, until it starts to turn golden brown. Sprinkle with the garlic and salt and continue to sauté for another 1 to 2 minutes, until fragrant and toasted. Remove from the heat and transfer to a paper towel–lined plate to drain any excess oil. Use as needed or store in an airtight container at room temperature for up to 4 days.

*Makes about 2 cups (185 g)*

# Pico de Gallo

*There is NOTHING sadder than store-bought pico. The tomatoes aren't flavorful or colorful, the onions aren't fresh, and the herbs are wilted. So just buck up and spend the five extra minutes to make your own—you'll thank me later.*

### Ingredients

1½ pounds (680 g) ripe tomatoes, cut into ¼- to ½-inch (6 to 12 mm) dice

½ large white onion, finely diced (about ¾ cup/95 g)

1 to 2 jalapeño chiles, finely diced (remove seeds and membranes for a milder salsa)

½ cup (20 g) finely chopped fresh cilantro leaves

1 tablespoon fresh lime juice
Kosher salt

In a large bowl, combine the tomatoes, onion, jalapeño, cilantro, and lime juice. Gently toss to combine. Taste and season with salt as needed. Add extra jalapeño if you want a bit more zip.

*Makes 4 cups  (800 g)*

# Gaby's Famous Guacamole

*Obviously mandatory. In addition to being a highly recommended topping for a number of recipes in this book, I think everyone should have their own signature guac recipe. This is a great start because it's—in my opinion—guacamole in its purest form. Just lemon and lime (trust me on that), chives (instead of cilantro), salt, and pepper. I'm not into garlic (sacrilege) or tomatoes in my guac, but sometimes I'll throw in a few tablespoons of Chipotle Salsa (page 252) if I want to add an extra kick.*

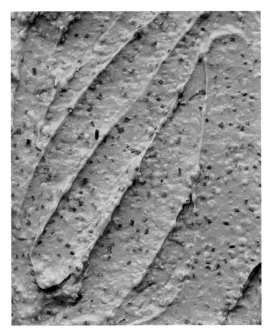

### Ingredients

4 ripe Hass avocados

Juice of 1 lemon, plus more if needed

Juice of 1 lime, plus more if needed

Kosher salt and freshly cracked black pepper

⅓ cup (40 g) finely chopped red onion

3 to 4 tablespoons (8 to 11 g) freshly chopped chives

2 teaspoons finely chopped jalapeño chile

Cut the avocados in half lengthwise. Remove the pit from the avocados and discard. Scoop out the avocado flesh and place into a bowl.

Add the lemon juice and lime juice and season with salt and pepper. Mash everything together with a fork until half smooth and creamy. Stir in the red onion, chives, and jalapeño. Taste, adjust the lemon and lime juice, and add more salt and pepper if desired. Serve immediately with tortilla chips.

*Make 1½ cups (350 g)*

# Index